Best Wishes for Stella.

Warm Regards

from Takao Mae

, July 2019

JAPAN'S WORLD HERITAGE SITES

UNIQUE CULTURE, UNIQUE NATURE

JOHN DOUGILL

TUTTLE Publishing

Tokyo | Rutland, Vermont | Singapore

Published by Tuttle Publishing, an imprint
of Periplus Editions (HK) Ltd.

www.tuttlepublishing.com

ISBN: 978-4-8053-1285-8

Distributed by
North America, Latin America & Europe
Tuttle Publishing
364 Innovation Drive
North Clarendon, VT 05759-9436 USA
Tel: 1 (802) 773-8930
Fax: 1 (802) 773-6993
info@tuttlepublishing.com
www.tuttlepublishing.com

Japan
Tuttle Publishing
Yaekari Building, 3rd Floor
5-4-12 Osaki
Shinagawa-ku
Tokyo 141-0032
Tel: (81) 3 5437-0171
Fax: (81) 3 5437-0755
sales@tuttle.co.jp
www.tuttle.co.jp

Asia Pacific
Berkeley Books Pte Ltd
61 Tai Seng Avenue, #02-12
Singapore 534167
Tel: (65) 6280-1330
Fax: (65) 6280-6290
inquiries@periplus.com.sg
www.periplus.com

17 16 15   10 9 8 7 6 5 4 3 2

Printed in Singapore   1506TW

PAGE 1 Kinkaku-ji, page 48.

PAGES 2/3 Mount Fuji, page 14.

RIGHT Heijo Palace, page 92.

Kinkaku-ji, page 48   Futarasan Shrine, page 144   Mount Fuji, page 14

CONTENTS

The Significance of Japan's World Heritage Sites   8

Itsukushima Shrine, page 20   The Ogasawara Islands, page166   Kumano, page 122

The Peace Memorial at Hiroshima, page 26   Toshodai-ji, page 108   Ginkaku-ji, page 56

Shirakawa-Go and Gokoyama, page 32   Kiyomizu-dera, page 40

Nijo Castle, page 44

The Significance of Japan's World Heritage Sites

A Personal Journey

In 2012, I set off to tour Japan's seventeen World Heritage sites, traveling the length of the country from the north of Hokkaido down to Okinawa. It was an auspicious year to do so. Not only was it the twentieth anniversary of Japan's first World Heritage registration but the fortieth anniversary of the UNESCO convention. By way of celebration, the organisation put on a conference in Kyoto, where I'm fortunate to live, and I was able to attend what the Director General of UNESCO called 'a unique gathering of the best minds in terms of World Heritage'—560 people from 60 countries.

Discussions at the conference centered around the successes and problems encountered during its four decades. In the twenty years from 1992, the number of sites had grown from 358 to 962. Of concern were such matters as how to judge universal value; how to ensure local involvement and benefit; how to safeguard against the destructive effects of tourism; and how to make sure that the concentration of resources on World Heritage Sites does not prove detrimental to others. The key word in all this was 'sustainability'.

But what of my journey? Japan is a surprisingly long country and the trip took over four months as I moved steadily southwards from the subarctic in Shiretoko down towards the subtropical in Okinawa and Ogasawara. Contrary to the popular notion of Japan as a place of overcrowded cities, the journey began and ended in remote areas of unspoilt nature. Few countries can be as pleasant to travel around as Japan, for its people are unfailingly polite and the transport system efficient and timely. Though public transport was my preferred option, car rental sometimes proved the only practical option.

Along the way there were plenty of adventures. In the mountainous Shirakami area of northern Honshu, my driver fell asleep at the wheel one afternoon, not only wrecking the car but managing to strand us in one of the few spots in Japan with no mobile access and no passing traffic. As midnight approached and we sat vainly trying to sleep in the wrecked vehicle, a flashing light split the darkness and a small police car arrived to tell us that we were camping illegally!

ABOVE During the time of the Ryukyu Kingdom, important state ceremonies were held in the inner compound of Okinawa's Shuri Castle, including the reception of foreign dignitaries.

RIGHT Massive pillars support the viewing platform of Kiyomizu Temple more than 40 feet (13 meters) above ground. In the Edo Period, devotees of Kannon would throw themselves off in the hope of winning spiritual merit.

There were other close encounters. At Shiretoko, the hiking group I was with almost came across two brown bears, a mother and her cub, said to be the most dangerous combination for humans. We thought we had steered well clear of them but had to think again when we came to a clearing with uprooted plants and a pungent smell. A few minutes earlier and we would have inadvertently stumbled upon them. Two days later, in Shirakami Sanchi, I did stumble upon a bear at the aptly named Black Bear Falls. It was coming round a bend in the path, and although the advice in such cases is not to panic, I was just about to run for my life when fortunately the bear beat me to it.

Sadly, it was not possible to do all the sites full justice, for hiking every single nature trail and pilgrimage route could take years. Moreover, there were times when it seemed that fate was determined to thwart me, for everywhere I went there was something under repair. This was sometimes due to the natural disasters that plague Japan. For instance, the pond garden at Hiraizumi had been damaged by an earthquake and the surrounds of the Nachi waterfall by a typhoon. But there

was a greater factor at play: of the 3,600 buildings in Japan designated as important cultural properties, 3,300 are wooden. When these ancient buildings need renewing, the repairs can be costly and time-consuming.

So which were my favorite sites? The biggest 'wow' came amidst the fabulous gnarled cedar trees of Yakushima even though I'd been to the island before and knew what to expect. Walking in the woods one early morning, I stood riveted to the spot as the sun came up over a hillside and a whole swathe of forest was slowly brought to life by its spreading rays. It was as if a black-and-white painting was being transformed before my very eyes into full color. Sheer magic!

The site that most took my fancy, however, was my final destination. It was quite literally 'a voyage of discovery', for the only way to Ogasawara is 25 hours by ship. It means that relatively few travel to the thinly populated islands despite the beauty of subtropical hillsides set amongst Pacific blues. They were registered with UNESCO because of the unusual life forms that have developed over the millennia, but for myself the history of the islands was no less alluring.

ABOVE Picturesque views of Mt Fuji have long proved a source of artistic and spiritual inspiration, prompting recognition of the volcano as a Cultural (rather than Natural) World Heritage.

ABOVE The bronze bell at Buddhist temples, such as this one at Kyoto's Enryaku-ji, can be heard for distances of up to 20 miles (32 km) and require great craftsmanship in casting, with a failure rate of nearly 50 percent.

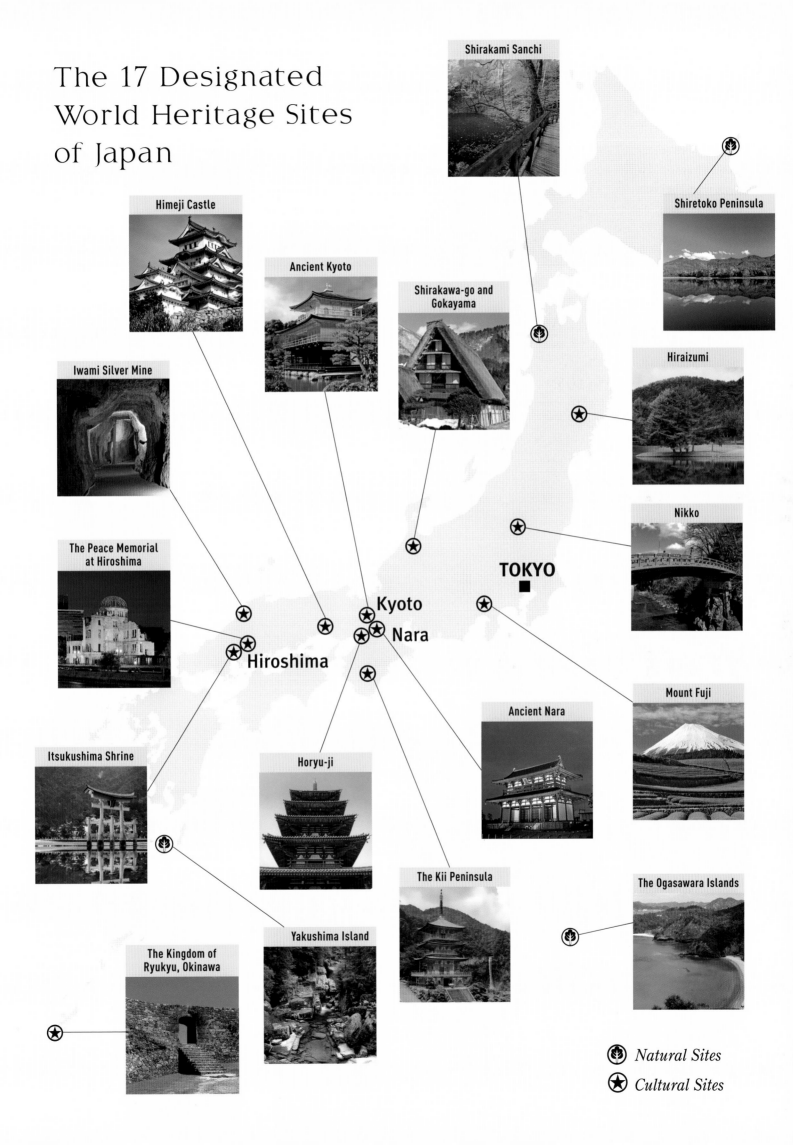

The 17 Designated World Heritage Sites of Japan

Shirakami Sanchi

Himeji Castle

Ancient Kyoto

Shirakawa-go and Gokayama

Shiretoko Peninsula

Iwami Silver Mine

Hiraizumi

The Peace Memorial at Hiroshima

Nikko

TOKYO

Kyoto

Nara

Hiroshima

Mount Fuji

Itsukushima Shrine

Horyu-ji

Ancient Nara

The Kii Peninsula

The Ogasawara Islands

The Kingdom of Ryukyu, Okinawa

Yakushima Island

🍃 *Natural Sites*
★ *Cultural Sites*

Until the 1840s Ogasawara was uninhabited. The archipelago was first settled by a group of Westerners and Pacific Islanders, some of whose descendants remain to this day. At one point, Britain and the United States were arguing over ownership, and only after the Meiji Restoration of 1868 did the islands become officially part of Japan. There is something of the charm of the southern seas about them. Perhaps it was the enchantment of distance, or perhaps it was simply because my journey was drawing to an end. Whatever the reason, Japan's most remote World Heritage Site turned out to be the nearest to my heart. You could say it was the one site that truly 'registered'.

Postscript

With the registration of Mount Fuji as a World Heritage site in the spring of 2013, I found myself adding an important postscript to my travels. Although I'd climbed the mountain in my younger days, I was unfamiliar with the many listed properties included by UNESCO as part of the site (25 in all). These concern the cultural and spiritual heritage of the mountain, involving some out-of-the-way places. So I rented a car and embarked on a two-day drive around the base of Fuji, which took me deep into rural Yamanashi with a side trip to the Shizuoka seaside for a celebrated view of the volcano. It was just a month after the official acceptance by UNESCO and there was a celebratory feel, with flags happily proclaiming the new status at all the key spots, indicative of a well-run campaign.

June and July are said to be the worst times of the year for Fuji-viewing because of the cloud cover, but I was lucky to see the sacred mountain basking in sunshine from several different angles. The inspiration Fuji provided for artists is one of the two pillars on which registration rested, the other being its religious aspect. Among the listed properties are shrines, springs, pathways and lodging houses for pilgrims. Religious rites were also carried out in lava caves formed around tree trunks which subsequently rotted away. The variety of Fuji's listed properties typify the wide-ranging appeal of Japan's World Heritage Sites as a whole, for while some are popular tourist sights, others involve exploration of little-known and rarely visited places. It was with a desire to communicate the wealth and diversity of such sites that I had set out on my journey in the first place. Japan has long had a reputation as the treasure house of Asia. My hope is that this book will not only help further awareness of its exceptional cultural heritage but also of the need for conservation of its remarkable natural heritage.

ABOVE The distinctive 'prayer-hand roofs' of Gokoyama village houses were designed to protect them from snow in winter and to provide space for cottage industries.

The World Heritage Sites Program

In 1972, UNESCO ratified a convention to further preservation of places of 'outstanding universal value' by awarding them the status of World Heritage. At the time of writing, there are 981 such sites, a number that is growing year by year. They are located in 160 countries and include some of the most famous places on earth, such as the Taj Mahal, the Statue of Liberty, the Tower of London, the Great Wall of China and the Galapagos Islands.

Nominations are put forward by signatory countries to the convention, and the sites are expected to meet a set of demanding criteria. There are two main categories: Cultural and Natural (some sites fall into both types and others are considered 'cultural landscapes'). A vetting process takes into consideration such matters as authenticity, management, accessibility and protection measures. Registration brings rewards in terms of pride, prestige and publicity, resulting in an increase in visitors.

Interest in World Heritage Sites is enormous in Japan, with specialist tours and television programs: TBS has shown a weekly documentary since 1996 and NHK has a partnership arrangement to co-produce videos for UNESCO's archives. It's surprising, then, that Japan has relatively few sites compared with its peers. As of 2013, it has a total of 17 compared to 19 for Australia, 21 for the USA, 28 for the UK, 38 each for Germany and France, 44 for Spain and 45 for China.

The numbers are misleading, however, for what defines a site can vary from a single building to a whole region. Several of Japan's sites boast multiple 'properties', some of which could easily stand as World Heritage Sites in their own right. Take Kyoto, for instance, which lists world-famous temples, gardens and even a castle amongst its 17 properties.

TOP Shinkyo Bridge at Nikko has mythological origins but took its present form in 1636. Once reserved for imperial messengers, it is now a popular place for wedding photos.

ABOVE The vermilion color of Japan's shrines, here seen at Kyoto's Shimogamo Jinja, originated in China and was transmitted via Buddhism to Japan.

TOP Nara's Kasuga Shrine has some 2,000 stone lanterns as well as a further 1,000 hanging lanterns. Twice a year, at Setsubun (February) and Obon (August), the lanterns are lit in a spectacular display.

ABOVE Hiking on Yakushima Island takes one deep into pristine forests with ancient cedar trees, some of which are thousands of years old.

MOUNT FUJI

JAPAN'S TALLEST MOUNTAIN
AND A SACRED SYMBOL OF THE NATION

**MOUNT FUJI
AT A GLANCE**

REGISTRATION 2013, as 'Mt Fuji: Object
of Worship, Wellspring of Art'.

FEATURES 25 properties in Shizuoka
and Yamanashi Prefectures, including the
summit (12,389 feet/3,776 meters), ascent
routes, 8 shrines, purification springs,
5 lakes, pilgrim lodging houses, caves,
a viewpoint and a waterfall.

ACCESS From Tokyo by train to Fujisan
Station (90 mins). The town of Fujiyoshida
is a good starting point.

DURATION There are 4 ascent routes, and
one can drive up to the 5th station (there
are 10 in all). Ascents take 4–8 hours
(typically with an overnight stay to see the
sunrise). Allow at least 2 days to drive
round Fuji to view the properties. Rental
car recommended.

FEES Most properties are free (a charge
is being considered for ascent of Mt Fuji).

INFORMATION Shizuoka World Heritage
division tel. (054) 221-3746. Yamanashi
World Heritage division tel. (055) 223-1316.
Volunteer guide for Lake Kawaguchi area:
ysgg_office@yahoo.co.jp. Wikitravel has a
comprehensive webpage. For a self-guided
tour from Tokyo, see the Fuji page of www.
go-japango.com.travel.

Symmetrical and snow-capped, Mt Fuji is an iconic symbol of Japan. Since ancient times it's been held in awe, and many Japanese harbor the desire to climb it at least once in their life. It was previously nominated as a Natural Heritage site but environmental problems necessitated rethinking the application as a Cultural Heritage site based on its religious and artistic significance.

Fuji's religious role stems from the country's animist tradition of mountain worship, prompted not only by its dominating presence but by its volcanic activity. Since 781 there have been 17 recorded eruptions, the last being in 1707, and to appease the mountain deity Sengen shrines were built around the base.

Of the eight shrines in the World Heritage registration, Fujisan Hongu Sengen Taisha is the most important. Established at its present location in 806, it boasts an unusual two-storey sanctuary as well as ponds fed by underground water from Mt Fuji. It stands at the head of some 1,300 Sengen shrines nationwide.

From the twelfth century, as volcanic activity lessened, the mountain became a base for mountain asceticism (*shugendo*), which mixes esoteric Buddhism with Taoism and worship of *kami* (divine spirits or Shino deities). 'Entering the mountain' is seen as a form of death and rebirth, by which the old self is killed off and the practitioner returns spiritually enhanced. After the fifteenth century, ordinary people became involved, led on pilgrimages by a *shugendo* practitioner. Around this time, the mountain deity became conflated with a mythological princess called Konohanasakuya-hime because of her association with beauty.

By the eighteenth century there was a flourishing Fuji-ko sect. The founder, Hasegawa Kakugyo (1541–1646), did austerities in a small cave at Hitoana, now a registered property, where he had a mystic vision of Fuji as the divine fount of life. Followers were encouraged to do ritualised pilgrimages, and stone markers record their names and the number of worship-ascents.

Amongst other Fuji sites listed with UNESCO are two 'lava mould caves' in which trees once covered by lava have rotted to form hollow openings. Here, within the 'womb' of Konohanasakuya-hime, sect members were symbolically reborn. Elsewhere, purification rites were performed at the Shiraito Falls and at the Oshino Hakkai Springs, fed by underground water from Fuji.

Fuji-ko members were organised into confraternities, for whom guides called Oshi facilitated arrangements. In the town of Fujiyoshida, there were once 86 Oshi lodging houses but today only a handful remain. Ascents of Fuji used to start from one of the Sengen shrines, though nowadays most of the 300,000 climbers drive up to the 5th station. The climbing season is July and August and at peak times, such as weekends, the trail is congested and mountain huts booked out.

Alongside its religious role, Mt Fuji has loomed large in the poetic imagination, inspiring medieval folk tales and the haiku of Matsuo Basho. Already in the eighth-century anthology *Manyoshu*, reference can be found to Fuji's divinity.

OPPOSITE Shizuoka tea fields ripen in the summer sunshine, while behind them snow covers the graceful slopes of Mt Fuji. The climbing season is limited to July and August when the snow has melted.

BELOW The replica of a sailing ship on which Europeans once traveled to Japan adds an exotic touch to viewing trips of Mt Fuji on Lake Ashi.

BELOW LEFT In the past, Fuji Sengen Jinja at Subarashi was one of the main starting points for ascent of the mountain. Extensively damaged by the eruption of 1707, it was rebuilt in 1718.

BELOW MIDDLE It's said that Kawaguchi Asama Shrine was built after eruptions in the ninth century to appease the mountain deity. In the late middle ages, the area became a center for guides called Oshi who led pilgrim-ascents of the volcano.

BELOW RIGHT Fujisan Hongu Sengen Taisha is notable for its distinctive architecture and pond fed by spring water from the mountain. It stands at the head of over 1,300 shrines nationwide dedicated to Mt Fuji.

ABOVE One of the fascinations of Fuji is that views can change dramatically, not only from season to season but even during the course of a single day.

RIGHT Watching the sunrise from the summit is the goal of many climbers, and Goraiko (the coming of light) above the clouds can be a magical experience, shared with hundreds of others.

RIGHT BOTTOM The volcanic slopes, devoid of vegetation, do not require special climbing skills but can be strenuous near the summit because of the thin air.

In the land of Yamato,
It is our treasure, our tutelary god.
It never tires our eyes to look up
To the lofty peak of Mount Fuji.

The mountain also has a long tradition of artistic representation, in which the Fuji Five Lakes play an important role. Scenic viewspots show Fuji's many guises reflected in the shimmering water, and a scene from Lake Motosu is printed on Japan's Y1000 note. Another viewpoint, 28 miles (45 km) away on the coast, is Miho no Matsubara which was popular in the past for Fuji sketches featuring the pines on its beach (associated with the Hagoromo legend about a feathered robe).

The most celebrated pictures, however, are the *ukiyo-e* paintings by Hokusai Katsushika and Hiroshige Utagawa, who both did *Thirty-six Views of Fuji*. The latter also produced a series of *Fifty-three Stations of the Tokaido*, which served to imprint the mountain on the modern consciousness, not only in Japan but abroad through its influence on Post-Impressionists. Once a feared volcano, the beauty of 'Fuji-san' now bewitches the wider world.

TOP In the past, Fuji could be seen from street level in Tokyo but nowadays views can only be had from observatories on the city's high-rise buildings.

ABOVE LEFT The Shiraito Falls at Fujinomiya, Shizuoka Prefecture, were sacred to the Fuji cult because the water comes from snowmelt of the divine mountain. The name means 'white thread', an apt description of the gushing wide arc of the waterfall.

ABOVE RIGHT Members of a group to secure World Heritage status for Mt Fuji give thanks for their success at Kitaguchi Hongu Fuji Sengen Shrine in Fujiyoshida.

OPPOSITE ABOVE The Fuji Five Lakes (Goko) offer some fine views, with 'reverse Fuji' reflections in the water particularly treasured. Lake Motosu, pictured here, is featured on Japan's Y1000 bank notes.

OPPOSITE BELOW Fishermen go about their work at Kumomi on the southeastern coast of Izu Peninsula, a popular tourist destination because of the views.

ITSUKUSHIMA SHRINE

THE QUINTESSENTIAL SYMBOL OF JAPAN

**ITSUKUSHIMA SHRINE
AT A GLANCE**

REGISTRATION 1996, for combining architecture with nature in 'a work of art of incomparable beauty'.

FEATURES A Shinto shrine in an inlet on the island of Miyajima, with 56 wooden structures supported by pillars and connected by corridors.

ACCESS From JR Hiroshima, 25 mins by train to JR Miyajimaguchi, then connecting ferry (10 mins) and 15 mins walk. A direct boat also leaves from Peace Park (55 mins).

PRACTICALITIES 6.30–17.30 (in season). Y300. Miyajima Tourist Association tel. (0829) 44 0066 (free guided tours, or email taif@fureai-ch.ne.jp 10 days in advance). For accommodation information, see the wikivoyage page on Miyajima.

DATELINE
Ancient times—Miyajima regarded as sacred
593—Shinto shrine erected
1168—Present layout established
1868—Shrine and temple buildings
  separated

Perhaps no other landmark represents Japan as eloquently as Itsukushima. The *torii* (Shinto gate) that stands in the sea has become an iconic image, evoking the harmony with nature that typifies traditional architecture. The shrine seems at high tide to be floating on the sea, and its vermilion structures are offset by the blue waters and mountain greenery that frame them. Form, color and composition here come together in a glowing example of sensitivity to place.

The shrine was laid out in its present form by a warlord named Taira no Kiyomori (1118–81), who ascribed his victories to the benevolence of the Itsukushima *kami* (divine spirit) The positioning in an inlet was unprecedented, and to explain it several theories have been put forward. One has to do with ensuring worshippers did not defile the sacred island by stepping ashore. Another involves recreation of the Dragon King's Palace of mythology. A third concerns representation of the Buddhist Pure Land (paradise), in fashion in Kiyomori's time, according to which those who died were conveyed across a stretch of water to a divine abode.

The style of architecture derived from the aristocratic villas of Kyoto. Known as *shinden-zukuri*, it involved a network of elegant and spacious rooms connected by wooden corridors. Integration into the surrounds was created through the use of natural materials, such as wood and cypress roof tiles. The villa rooms featured views onto specially designed pond gardens, which are here replaced by the sea and the shoreline opposite.

RIGHT Viewed from the beach at low tide, the shrine offers a scene of pleasing elegance. Prominent on the hill behind is a five-storey Buddhist pagoda and the huge 1,000-mat Hall.

OPPOSITE Itsukushima's 'floating *torii*' was first erected in 1168 to welcome pilgrims arriving by boat. Last renewed in 1875, it is made from decay-resistant camphor wood.

The most famous of the structures, the Great Torii, stands 52 feet (16 meters) high and weighs about 60 tons. Its purpose was to welcome worshippers who would have originally arrived at the shrine by boat. (The buildings are similarly aligned, with the altar facing towards holy Mt Misen on the island behind.) The *torii* was last rebuilt in 1875, and the giant pillars are made from camphor trees 500–600 years old. Such is the tidal difference that at low tide it is possible to walk out to inspect them, while at high tide one can sail through.

Within the shrine complex is an assortment of subshrines as well as three different stages. One is a long stage for ceremonies, one a high stage for stately court dances and one a Noh stage—the only one in the world to be set upon the sea. It had to be specially adapted, as indeed did the corridors through the addition of gaps between floorboards to allow for the rising tide.

Included in the World Heritage listing are peripheral buildings, such as two striking pagodas. Interestingly, these are Buddhist, for like other religious complexes Itsukushima followed a fusion of Shinto-Buddhism until the Meiji Restoration of 1868, when the government forcibly separated the two religions. Several buildings were destroyed in the process, but the pagodas survived as did another World Heritage property, the Senjokaku (the 1,000-mat Hall). Though

it was built for the chanting of Buddhist sutras, it serves now as a shrine to the soul of its founder, Toyotomi Hideyoshi (1536–98).

For those with time to spare, staying overnight is recommended for it allows visitors to savor the atmosphere once the crowds have gone. It also enables visitors to see the shrine in two different guises, at low and high tide. There are plenty of attractions, as typically for a Japanese

pilgrimage site there's a vibrant area of shops offering souvenirs and refreshments. There's also a ropeway up Mt Misen; a night cruise to the *torii*; and hundreds of deer that pose for photographs (the animals are regarded as messengers of the *kami*). For those visiting in late July, there's a floating festival when decorated shrine boats are joined by hundreds of lantern-lit fishing vessels—quintessential Japan, indeed.

Itsukushima Shrine

1. Soribashi (Arched Bridge or Imperial Messenger's Bridge)
2. Nishi Kairo (West Corridor)
3. Noh Stage
4. Tenjin Shrine
5. Kadomarodo Shrine
6. Hitasaki (Front lantern)
7. Takabutai (High Stage)
8. Hirabutai (Flat Stage)
9. Haraiden (Purification Hall)
10. Haiden (Worship Hall)
11. Honden (Sanctuary)
12. Marodo Shrine
13. Higashi Kairo (East Corridor)

FAR LEFT At low tide it's possible to walk out to the *torii*, where people place coins in the cracks of the pillars for good luck or gather shellfish to eat at home.

MIDDLE LEFT The architectural style, with its roofed corridors, was inspired by the aristocratic palaces of the Heian Period, which overlooked pond gardens.

LEFT Since medieval times, nearby streets have catered to throngs of pilgrim-tourists for whom hunting for souvenirs is part of the experience.

BELOW The connecting corridors that run between the shrine's structures have gaps between the floorboards to relieve pressure from the rising water during high tide.

FOLLOWING SPREAD Despite the advent of modern tourism, the island is still considered sacred and to avoid 'pollution' births, deaths and burials take place on the mainland.

THE PEACE MEMORIAL AT HIROSHIMA

SOLE SURVIVOR OF THE WORLD'S FIRST NUCLEAR BLAST

On August 6, 1945, at 8.15 am, the world's first nuclear bombing occurred. The explosion took place 1,968 feet (600 meters) above Hiroshima's commercial center, flattening the whole district. The sole structure left standing was the skeletal remains of a building which came to be known as the Genbaku Dome (Atomic Bomb Dome). In 1966, a resolution was passed by Hiroshima City Council to preserve it in perpetuity.

Designed by a Czech architect, the brick building had a five-storey core capped by a copper-clad dome. When the bomb exploded, the main structure shattered but miraculously the iron-framed dome held in place. It's the only building to remain from the time of the blast, and it acts as the focal point for the Peace Memorial Park and Museum which attract nearly a million and a half visitors every year.

In the park are monuments to those who died. There's a burial mound with the ashes of 70,000 unidentified victims, and a cenotaph listing everyone who perished as a result of the blast at the time or later (some 200,000). There's also a monument for the Korean victims, many of whom were conscripts. Most famously

RIGHT Schoolchildren pay respects to the monument for twelve-year-old Sadako Sasaki, behind which hang hundreds of paper cranes in her memory.

of all, there's a memorial to twelve-year-old Sadako Sasaki, who believed that if she folded 1,000 cranes she would be cured of radiation illness.

The Peace Memorial Museum is divided into two parts. The East Building tells the story of Hiroshima before and after the bombing. The West Building focusses on the physical effects. Some of the exhibits are heart-rending: clothing remnants, charred lunch boxes, the last words of dying children. Details of the destruction are portrayed through photos and paintings. Black rain streaks cover a white plaster wall and the stages of radiation sickness are graphically displayed. It's a moving experience designed to reinforce the exhibition's central message: Never again!

TOP The Peace Memorial building was designed in 1915 by a Czech architect as part of the Hiroshima Prefectural Commercial Exhibition. The only structure left standing near the epicenter of the nuclear explosion, it is widely known as the Genbaku Dome (Atomic Bomb Dome).

ABOVE The Peace Bell sounds mournfully throughout the Memorial Park as visitors line up to ring it. Constructed in 1964, it bears a map of the world and an atomic symbol marks the spot where it is struck.

HIMEJI CASTLE

JAPAN'S BEST-PRESERVED SAMURAI STRONGHOLD

**HIMEJI CASTLE
AT A GLANCE**

REGISTRATION 1993, for combining
military function with aesthetic appeal.

FEATURES Castle with 2 moats (originally
3) and 83 structures arranged around a
6-storey tower.

PRACTICALITIES Access from Himeiji JR
stn (15 mins walk). Open 9.00–17.00 (last
entry 16.00). Y400. Volunteer guides available
through Information Office or try himejitour-
kashinoki@gmail.com. Guided tours take
90 mins.

INFORMATION Tourist Information Office
at JR station (079) 222-0003; email: info@
himeji.kanko.jp Castle tel. (079) 285-1146.

DATELINE
1333—First hill fortification
1581—Remodeled by Toyotomi Hideyoshi
1601–9—Present layout adopted
1618—Extra buildings added
1871—Sold at auction
1930—Parts designated as National Treasure

Of the twelve castles which remain intact
from Japan's samurai age, Himeiji is the
biggest and best preserved. It combines a
sophisticated defence system with beauty
of design, such that it has been compared
to a bird taking flight (hence the nick-
name, the White Egret Castle). It was
built on a grand scale yet with sensitivity
to the landscape, as a result of which it
appears integrated into nature. It seems
extraordinary that this robust complex
was made from only the simplest of
natural materials: wood, water, stone
and clay.

The proportions of the castle are
staggering. It is fifty times larger than the
Tokyo Dome and the combined length
of the walls totals three miles (4.8 km).
The tallest section is 85 feet (26 meters)
high, built entirely without mortar so as

to allow for earthquakes. When the
builders ran short of stone, they resorted
to tombstones, coffins and temple
lanterns, some of which can be seen in
the fabric of the wall. Also visible is a
small grinding stone which belonged to a
widow who was moved by the shortage to
donate her precious kitchen implement.
It prompted other donations and helped
speed up the construction.

Every aspect of the castle was built with
defence in mind. The network of storehouses and residences was arranged in
a maze-like manner so as to confuse
attackers, and even today with signboards
pointing the way tourists can find the
layout baffling. The 84 gates of the
original castle (only 21 remain) were
designed to channel attackers into a spiral
of narrow passages where they could be

RIGHT A man in samurai uniform poses at the entrance
to the castle grounds. There were originally three moats
but only the inner and parts of the central moat have
survived.

OPPOSITE The magnificent main keep of the castle has
undergone an extensive five-year restoration, which
involved replastering the walls and replacing the roof tiles.
The tower appears to have five floors, but there is actually
a disguised sixth floor and a basement.

RIGHT The grounds of the castle are well known for cherry blossom viewing, and in early April there's a festival with lantern illumination culminating in a performance of drums and some 100 kimono-clad harpists.

BELOW Beneath the multistoreyed tower stands one of the original 84 gates. The castle boasts formidable defences but was never, in fact, tested in battle.

shot at from above. The castle walls have roughly 1,000 loopholes—circular, triangular and rectangular—from which rifles and arrows could be fired.

Some of the design details are ingenious. The castle walls are coated with white plaster that was resistant to fire, and one of the moats served as a water reserve for fire-fighting purposes. Windows have bars that look like wood but are actually metal to prevent them being sawn through. They are also hollow inside to allow for drainage of rainwater from the roofs. The long corridors have concealed openings for rocks or boiling liquid to be dropped on attackers, while guardrooms were designed to enable ambushes. If all else failed, a special area was reserved for hara-kiri.

The centerpiece of the castle is a 150-foot (46-meter) main tower, which effectively doubles the height of the hill on which it stands. From the outside it seems

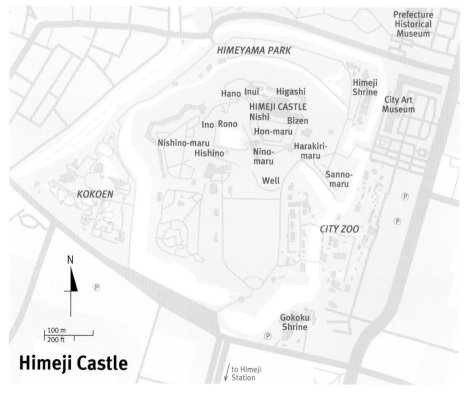

Himeji Castle

castles were destroyed as a legacy of feudalism, but it survived the plans of a property developer to demolish it and the bombing of the surrounds in World War II; a bomb landed but didn't explode. It also survived the destructive force of the Great Hanshin Earthquake of 1995.

An extensive five-year restoration program, due for completion in 2014, means that the castle will continue to be one of Japan's great treasures, recognised by UNESCO for its exceptional historical and aesthetic value. More than simply a castle, it constitutes a masterpiece of construction which serves as tribute to the prowess of its makers. Small wonder then that it has been a favorite for film makers, including famously the James Bond movie *You Only Live Twice* (1967) as well as Akira Kurosawa's samurai classic *Ran* (1985). Though its military use is over, Himeji Castle represents a shining showcase of Japan's pre-industrial achievements.

RIGHT ABOVE The connecting corridors that run along the castle walls look innocent enough but conceal ambush rooms and holes for dropping rocks on attackers.

RIGHT BELOW The approach to the castle leads round bends and curves in a maze-like manner, exposing would-be attackers to the mercy of defenders.

to have five floors but, in fact, it has six plus a basement (the fourth and fifth floors are constructed to appear as one). The structure is strengthened by two massive wooden pillars which stand on a stone foundation, and from the top are commanding views that on a clear day extend as far as the islands in the Inland Sea.

The castle's formidable defences were never put to the test, for they were constructed at the beginning of the long period of Tokugawa stability which lasted until the mid-nineteenth century. Yet the castle's survival today is a minor miracle, for it not only remained intact through Meiji-era modernisation when other

SHIRAKAWA-GO AND GOKOYAMA

TRADITIONAL MOUNTAIN VILLAGES
PRESERVING AN AGE-OLD WAY OF LIFE

SHIRAKAWA-GO AND GOKOYAMA AT A GLANCE

REGISTRATION 1995, as the 'Historic villages of Shirakawa-go and Gokoyama'.

FEATURES 3 villages comprising Ogimachi in Shirakawa-go, Gifu Prefecture, as well as Ainokura and Sugunuma in Gokoyama, Toyama Prefecture, 31 miles (50 km) to the north.

ACCESS From Takayama in Gifu Prefecture, 50 mins by bus to Ogimachi. From Kanazawa in Ishikawa Prefecture, 75 mins by bus. Rental car recommended for the Gokoyama villages.

DURATION By car the villages can be comfortably visited in a day. Opportunities to stay overnight (see japan-guide.com).

INFORMATION Shirakawa village office (05769) 6-1311; fax (05769) 6-1709; e-mail: hidatio@hidanet.ne.jp

ATTRACTIONS Museums, gift shops, open houses and viewing spots.

Deep in the mountains of central Japan is a remote river valley famous for its 'prayer-hand houses' (*gassho zukuri*). The name derives from the steeply angled roofs, which resemble hands joined together in Buddhist prayer. They are designed to cope with the weight of snow in winter, for the area has one of the heaviest snowfalls in Japan. As 95 per-cent of the area is mountainous, it meant that for long months in the past the villagers were cut off from the outside world. To cope, they developed a self-sufficient lifestyle for which the housing was indispensable.

Beneath the huge roofs are two-, three- and even four-storey houses. Remarkably, they are built without nails or metal supports, using only natural materials: wood, clay, straw and paper. An 'A frame' of giant oaks supports the roof, with the rafters bound in place by thick straw rope. The roof is covered with thatch, up to a meter thick, which has to be periodically renewed. Because of the risk of rotting, the re-thatching is carried out by a cooperative of forty or more villagers in just a single day or two.

The imposing structures could shelter extended families, with the largest holding up to around fifty people. The open hearths on the ground floor helped warm the upper levels, and the smoke served to repel insects and preserve the woodwork. The large roof space provided room for cottage industries, which compensated for the lack of income from arable land. Silkworm cultivation, the making of *washi* (Japanese paper) and the production of saltpeter for gun-powder helped sustain the households.

Sericulture, which required open space for silkworm beds and the storage of mulberry, took place on the upper floors,

RIGHT Traditional footwear in the deep snow of winter was a simple pair of straw boots.

FAR RIGHT The steeply pitched thatched roofs have large windows in the gable-end walls, designed to provide lighting and ventilation for silkworm production.

OPPOSITE Surrounded by mountains, the villagers were cut off in winter and the communities developed their own customs, social systems and folklore. Not only is the snow heavy and wet, but the area has one of the largest snowfalls in Japan.

where a gable window provided light and air. Excrement from the silkworms was used in the making of gunpowder, which was carried out on the lower levels, with the saltpeter being stored for safety in a hollow beneath the ground floor.

There were once some 1,800 prayer-hand houses but during the twentieth century numbers fell dramatically. By the 1960s there were only a few hundred left. Saltpeter and paper production ceased to be commercially viable in the late nineteenth century, and a hundred years later later silk production was in crisis. Households modernised or moved away, while dam developments put paid to whole villages. Only a concerted con-servation movement by residents of Ogimachi was able to halt the process, and houses under threat elsewhere were relocated to the community. Now, the World Heritage listing comprises 59 prayer-hand houses in Ogimachi, 20 in Ainokura and 9 in Sugunuma. Also listed are associated shrines, temples, groves and storehouses.

OPPOSITE ABOVE AND BELOW Ogimachi, largest of the World Heritage villages, has a nearby hill with a viewing area which is popular with tourists. Of the 152 households, 59 are 'prayer-hand houses' subject to conservation, along with temple buildings, storehouses and canals. Some of the traditional houses are open to the public, either as museums or as places to stay overnight.

RIGHT ABOVE Some of the houses are 300 years old. The construction of the frame was done by skilled professionals, but the roof structure was usually put up by the villagers themselves working together in a mutual self-help association.

RIGHT BELOW The large attic spaces were ideal for the silkworm beds necessary for sericulture. Notice the straw rope tightly bound around the roof supports; no nails were used.

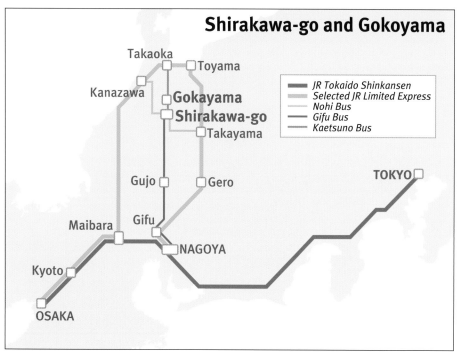

Shirakawa-go and Gokoyama

Takaoka

Toyama

Kanazawa

Gokayama

Shirakawa-go

Takayama

	JR Tokaido Shinkansen
	Selected JR Limited Express
	Nohi Bus
	Gifu Bus
	Kaetsuno Bus

Gujo   Gero

Gifu

TOKYO

Maibara

NAGOYA

Kyoto

OSAKA

ABOVE The two small World Heritage villages in Gokoyama have fewer visitors and retain more of a traditional atmosphere.

LEFT From Tokyo to Takayama, it takes 4.5 hours by train, and from there another 50 minutes by bus to reach Ogimachi (Shirakawa-go). From Tokyo to Kanazawa, it takes around 4 hours by train, followed by 75 minutes by bus. (Some buses require reservation.) In summer, buses running between Nagoya and Kanazawa also stop at Ogimachi.

With the loss of traditional means of support, many of the prayer-houses these days are open to the public. There are guest houses, shops, restaurants and museums of all types. Some museums display the lifestyle of former times while others focus on the tools and production methods of the cottage industries: silkworm beds, materials for saltpeter, the stages of paper making. There's also an open-air museum at Ogimachi which consists of traditional housing complete with waterwheel and a prayer-hand shrine. Because of the isolation, the area developed a distinctive style of folk song and dance, and these are featured at a museum in Gokoyama.

The houses themselves, however, remain the prime attraction with their long wooden floors, open hearths and the beauty of the rice rope wrapped around the rafters. They display a keen sense of craftsmanship. The giant oak beams, for instance, were chosen from trunks that had curved with the weight of snow, because the wood would be sturdier and more resilient, while the buildings were

constructed with a flexibility that allowed for earthquakes and severe weather. Built for the most part by simple villagers, the houses stand tribute to the affinity with nature that characterised the lifestyle of past generations in this remote area. In the words of the World Heritage citation, they are 'outstanding examples of a traditional way of life perfectly adapted to the environment'.

ABOVE Thatching the prayer-hand roofs is a huge undertaking. Traditionally, villagers would form collectives to complete the job in a day or two, so as to avoid damp getting into the straw. Nowadays, extendable aluminum ladders have replaced simple wooden ones.

BELOW On the ground floor are large hearths that are not only used for cooking but to warm the upper floors. The smoke also acts as a preservative for the wooden building.

WORLD HERITAGE SITES OF ANCIENT KYOTO

The Cultural Heartland of Japan

Kyoto was the capital of Japan for over 1,000 years and in its river basin was fostered much of the country's traditional culture: courtly aesthetics, Zen, Noh, the tea ceremony, kabuki, ikebana and the geisha arts. It is truly one of the world's great cities, recognised by UNESCO with its registration of 17 separate properties (it could have been so many more!).

'Kyoto embodies all the values that UNESCO treasures,' says Director General Irina Bokova. 'It is blessed by glorious nature. It has many intangible assets, like the Gion Festival. And it has wonderful people.'

Geographically speaking, three of the properties lie outside Kyoto City. The temple of Enryaku-ji lies in Otsu City, while Byodo-in and Ujigami Shrine are in the small town of Uji. Historically, however, they are firmly part of Kyoto culture.

In all, the site boasts over 200 buildings and gardens of high artistic merit. Here are places for which people fly across the seas: the Golden and Silver Pavilions, Nijo castle, Kiyomizu Temple, the world's most famous rock garden. Here are the quintessential elements of a culture that has enriched the world. Here, quite simply, is the glittering heart of Japan.

REGISTRATION 1994, as 'Historic Monuments of Ancient Kyoto (Kyoto, Uji and Otsu Cities)'.

FEATURES 17 properties, comprising 13 Buddhist temples, 3 Shinto shrines and 1 castle.

ACCESS Kyoto is 1 hour 15 mins from Kansai Airport or 2 hours 15 mins from Tokyo by bullet train. Public transport within the city can take time, so a geographical approach is advised (see map).

PRACTICALITIES Tourist information: Kyoto Station bldg 2F, tel. (075) 343-0548. Both Kyoto City and Kyoto Prefecture have English websites with sections on World Heritage Sites. Other useful websites: kyoto-magonote.jp; www.kyotoguide.com; www.kyoto.travel. For volunteer guides, see the list on JNTO's website.

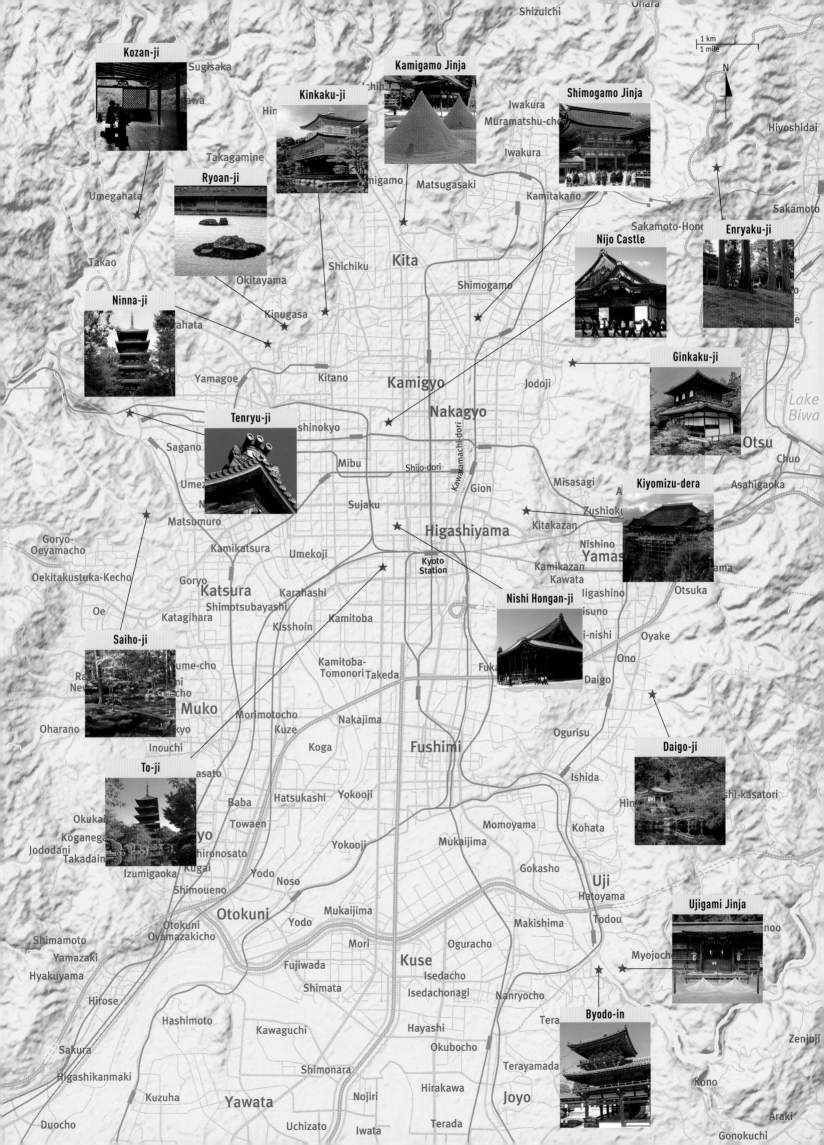

Kozan-ji

Kinkaku-ji

Kamigamo Jinja

Shimogamo Jinja

Ryoan-ji

Shimogamo Jinja

Nijo Castle

Enryaku-ji

Ninna-ji

Ginkaku-ji

Tenryu-ji

Kiyomizu-dera

Nishi Hongan-ji

Saiho-ji

Daigo-ji

To-ji

Ujigami Jinja

Byodo-in

Sugisaka

Takagamine

Umegahata

Takao

Hin

Kamigamo

Iwakura

Muramatsu-cho

Iwakura

Matsugasaki

Kamitakano

Shichiku

Kamitakano

Sakamoto-Hon

Sakamoto

Hiyoshidai

Okitayama

Kinugasa

Kitano

Shimogamo

Jodoji

Yamagoe

Kita

shinokyo

Kamigyo

Nakagyo

Sagano

Mibu

Shijo-dori

Kawaamachi-dori

Gion

Otsu

Chuo

Lake Biwa

Umez

Sujaku

Higashiyama

Misasagi

Asahigaoka

Matsumuro

Kyoto Station

Zushiok

Kitakazan

Nishino

Yamas

Goryo-Oeyamacho

Kamikatsura

Umekoji

Kamikazan

Kawata

Oekitakustuka-Kecho

Goryo

Katsura

Karahashi

ligashino

isuno

i-nishi

Oyake

Oe

Shimotsubayashi

Kamitoba

Ono

Katagihara

Kisshoin

Daigo

Ra

New

ume-cho

cho

Morimotocho

Nakajima

Ogurisu

Oharano

kyo

Kuze

Koga

Fushimi

Muko

Inouchi

Fuka

Izumigaoka

asato

Morimotocho-Tomonori

Takeda

Ishida

Hini

shi-kasatori

Okukai

Baba

Yokooji

Koganega

Towaen

Momoyama

Kohata

Jododani

hironosato

Kugai

Mukaijima

Gokasho

Uji

Takadain

Shimoueno

Yodo

Noso

Hatoyama

Myojoch

noo

Otokuni

Mukaijima

Todou

Shimamoto

Otokuni

Yodo

Mori

Oguracho

Yamazaki

Oyamazakicho

Fujiwada

Kuse

Isedacho

Nanryocho

Tera

Hyakuyama

Shimata

Isedachonagi

Hayashi

Terayamada

Zenjoji

Hirose

Kawaguchi

Okubocho

Kono

Sakura

Shimonara

Hirakawa

Joyo

Higashikanmaki

Nojiri

Terada

Araki

Kuzuha

Yawata

Uchizato

Iwata

Gonokuchi

Duocho

1 km
1 mile

N

KIYOMIZU-DERA

TEMPLE OF THE 'PURE WATER' SPRING AND KYOTO'S PREMIER PILGRIMAGE SITE

FEATURES A Kita-Hosso sect temple set on a hillside and famous for its viewing platform and Otowa Spring. Also includes the Jishu Shrine.

ACCESS From Kyoto JR stn, 15 mins by bus to Kiyomizu-michi or Gojo-zaka and 10 mins walk. Alternatively, 20 mins walk from Kiyomizu-Gojo stn on the Keihan line.

PRACTICALITIES 6.00–18.00. Y300. Temple tel. 075-551-1234. Allow up to 2 hours.

EVENTS Spring and autumn illumination 18.30–21.30. Y400.

DATELINE
778—Founded by Enchin Shonin
794—Founding of Heian-kyo (Kyoto)
1629—Fire destroys buildings incl. Main Hall
1633—Rebuilding and pagoda added

OPPOSITE TOP Schoolchildren pose in front of the fifteenth-century Niomon Gate, renovated in 2003. To the right is the Saimon (West Gate) and the Sanjunoto (three-storey pagoda).

OPPOSITE BOTTOM The platform of the Hondo (Main Hall) extends over a steep slope and is supported by 139 pillars. It is known as the Butai (Dance Stage) because performances were held there. Unlike the other temple buildings which are tiled, the Main Hall has a cypress bark roof to signify its palatial origins. The massive building extends for 190 feet (58 meters) and faces south, offering expansive views over its wooded surrounds and westwards towards the city.

Kiyomizu is Kyoto's premier tourist attraction. Along with its remarkable overhang architecture are spacious grounds, fine views, a 'love shrine' and a spring with magical properties (the temple's name means 'Pure Water'). The crowded approach, which leads up a slope along a narrow street of shops selling souvenirs and delicacies, is much in keeping with the past when pilgrim-tourists thronged the city's temples. It lends the magnificent World Heritage buildings a vibrant, bustling atmosphere. (Those who seek peace are advised to go at six in the morning.)

The temple originated in 778 when a Nara priest known as Enchin Shonin had a vision in which the whereabouts of the Otowa Spring was revealed to him. Twenty years later, in gratitude for his victories in the north, the 'barbarian-subduing generalissimo' Sakanoue no Tamuramaro donated a large hall which had originated as a palace building of Emperor Kammu. It was used to house an image of the 1,000-armed Kannon (deity of compassion) carved by Enchin.

In later centuries, the temple had to be rebuilt on numerous occasions due to damage by fire or fighting, and the present buildings are nearly all from a 1630s reconstruction. One exception is the fifteenth-century Niomon Gate, with its huge and fearsome protectors.

The Main Hall, unusually, has a shingled rather than a tiled roof because of its predecessor's imperial origins. Inside can be found an outer sanctuary with wooden paintings and an inner sanctuary with religious statuary,

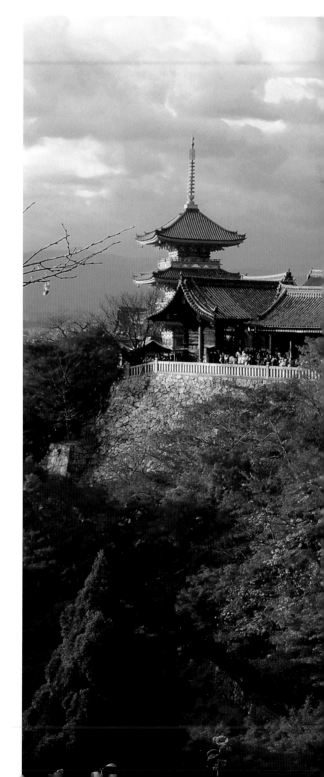

including Enchin's statue of Kannon which is only displayed once every 33 years.

The famous platform rests on giant pillars strategically positioned on a steep slope, and not a single nail was used in the construction. It offers fine views over the south of Kyoto, seasonally enhanced by cherry blossoms and autumn colors. There is a drop of 43 feet (13 meters), and in Edo times believers in Kannon would throw themselves off in the hope that their wishes would be granted. Astonishingly, of the 234 recorded incidents 85 percent survived, presumably thanks to the vegetation. It gave rise to a popular expression 'to jump off the Kiyomizu stage', meaning to take the plunge. (The practice was banned in 1872.)

Beyond the hall is the temple's guardian shrine, Jishu Jinja. Though officially separated from the temple after the Meiji Restoration of 1868, it is physically part of the complex and included in the Heritage registration. The shrine is particularly popular with young women since it enshrines the deity of match-making, and it is said that those who can walk with their eyes closed between two 'love stones' 59 feet (18 meters) apart will succeed in finding a partner.

There are several other structures in the temple grounds, some of which are only open for viewing on special occasions. These include the Jeju-in garden with its 'borrowed scenery', the Koyasu Pagoda associated with easy childbirth, and the Okunoin, a smaller version of the Main Hall with a similar platform. But the main attraction is undoubtedly the Otowa Spring, which flows out of the hillside and is the very source of the temple.

In Edo times, the spring was a popular place of pilgrimage due to belief in the curative qualities of the water. It falls in three separate streams, which according

to tradition represent health, longevity and success in exams. Science has proved the water to be pure, and visitors queue up to catch it in metal cups on long poles. (It is held to be greedy to drink from more than one stream.)

The route past the spring leads back to the entrance area, and those looking for closure might want to seek out the intriguing Zuiguido Hall, dedicated to Buddha's mother, where for Y100 you can enter pitch blackness and feel your way around a basement symbolising the womb. In this way, Kyoto's premier World Heritage Site will leave you with a sense of being 'reborn' and ready to explore the stores along the attractive alleys of Ninenzaka and Sannenzaka. As for the pilgrim-tourists of old, religion and recreation still go hand in hand.

ABOVE The Koyasu Pagoda, set in Kiyomizu's spacious grounds, is traditionally a place to pray for easy childbirth. Built in the seventeenth century, it stands in the south and faces towards the Hondo (Main Hall).

BELOW LEFT The temple honors a 'hidden Buddha' (*hibutsu*), which is only revealed every 33 years. The 11-headed, 1,000-armed statue of Kannon is said to have been carved by the founder, Enchin.

BELOW RIGHT Dressing in traditional style remains popular with young females, who like to visit the Love Shrine as well as to take the curative waters of the Otawa Spring.

NIJO CASTLE

SYMBOL OF THE TOKUGAWA SHOGUNATE'S POWER AND INFLUENCE IN OLD KYOTO

NIJO CASTLE AT A GLANCE

FEATURES Moated castle with 3 main areas: Ninomaru Palace, Hinomaru inner compound and encircling gardens.

ACCESS From Kyoto JR stn, 15 mins by taxi or 20 mins by city bus 9, 50 or 101.

PRACTICALITIES 8.45–16.00 (gate closes 17.00). Y600. Closed Tuesdays in July, Aug, Dec, Jan. Audio guide Y500. Castle office tel. (075) 841-0096; fax (075) 802-6181. Allow up to 2 hours for a visit.

EVENTS
March–April: Cherry blossom (over 400 trees)
Early Aug: Tanabata Festival and illumination
Mid-Oct–Nov: Castle festival

DATELINE
1603—Construction by Tokugawa Ieyasu
1626—Addition by Tokugawa Iemitsu of Ninomaru Palace
1867—Tokugawa Yoshinobu cedes castle to the emperor
1939—Emperor donates castle to the city of Kyoto

From 1603 to 1867, Japan was ruled by Tokugawa shoguns who lived in Edo (modern-day Tokyo). Nijo Castle was their base in Kyoto, serving as a reminder to the emperor in the nearby Imperial Palace of the shogunate's watchful eyes. It is not so much for its military function that the castle is admired, however, but for the lavishly decorated palace that lies within. The rooms there speak even more eloquently of Tokugawa power than the mighty walls that surround them.

The castle was erected in 1603 by the founding figure of the dynasty, Tokugawa Ieyasu. It was enlarged and completed by his grandson Iemitsu, who relocated items from Fushimi Castle built by Toyotomi Hideyoshi. These included a massive five-storey tower, which afforded views over the imperial palace until it burnt down in 1750. By that time, Tokugawa rule was so stable that reconstruction was considered unnecessary. The ruined steps of the tower can, however, still be seen today.

The layout of the castle comprises two concentric rings within an outer and

RIGHT The bridge over the inner moat connects the Ninomaru Palace area with the Honmaru (main enclosure).

FAR RIGHT The view from the Donjon (the keep) looks across the castle's spacious grounds towards Mt Hiei and the Eastern Hills. In total, the castle measures 1,640 feet (500 meters) by 1,312 feet (400 meters).

OPPOSITE TOP LEFT The Karamon (Chinese-style gate), brought here from Fushimi Castle, has a curved cypress bark roof above carvings of auspicious items.

OPPOSITE TOP RIGHT Schoolchildren file past the entrance to the Ninomaru Palace, beyond which is a series of five lavishly decorated buildings with a total of 33 rooms.

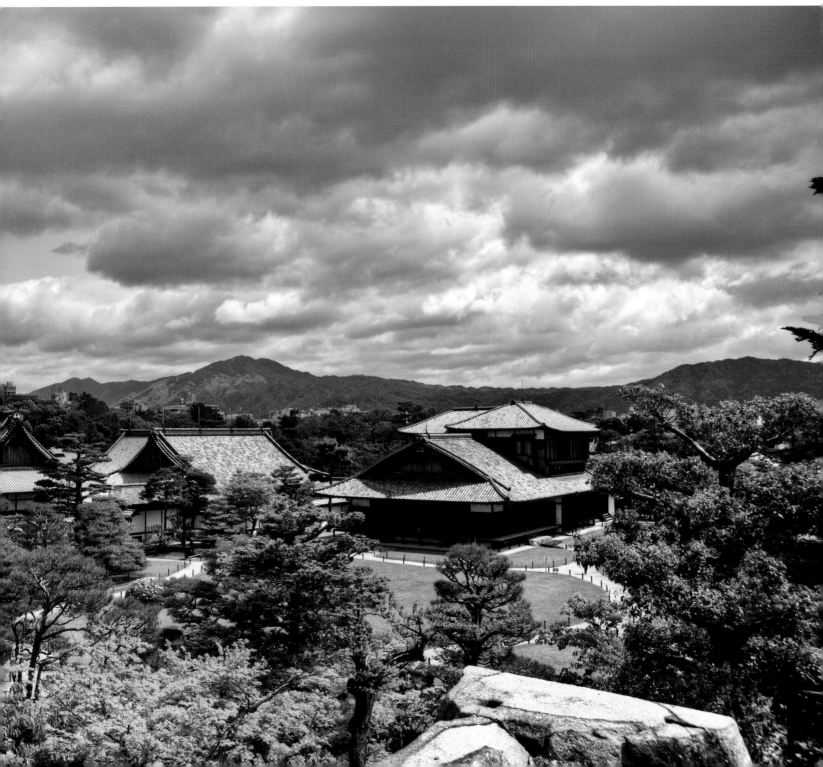

LEFT ABOVE The Ninomaru Palace buildings extend in zig-zag form towards the pond garden in structures that seem separate but are connected by corridors. In the distance, the Shiro Shoin once housed the private rooms of the shogun.

LEFT BELOW The Seiryu-en Garden on the north side of the castle was created in 1965 and has over a thousand rocks in all.

Outer Lords, while the fourth was for trusted allies of the shogun known as Inner Lords. (It was in one of the rooms here that the fifteenth Tokugawa shogun, Yoshinobu, signed his resignation in 1867, bringing to an end the shogunate form of government and marking the birth of modern Japan.) The fifth and final area was the shogun's private area, in which only female attendants were allowed.

The decor throughout is tailored to the room: intimidating images in the outer chambers, large-scale pines to suggest grandeur in the audience rooms, gentle landscapes in the residential quarters. The painters were directed by Kano Tanyu, top artist of the age, and in one famous picture a hawk surveys its surrounds as if the eyes of the shogunate were surveying the land. (Over 1,000 paintings are currently being replaced by replicas. The originals are occasionally displayed in a special gallery.)

inner moat. Visitors enter over the outer moat and through the eastern gate, passing before a guardhouse with figures dressed in period costume. A Chinese-style gate brought from Fushimi Castle gives onto the Ninomaru Palace, highlight of the visit. It consists of five connected buildings, made almost entirely from cypress, which are arranged in staggered form like the formation of geese in flight. The Nightingale Corridors, popular with tourists, have an inbuilt alarm system by which the floorboards squeak when anyone approaches.

There are 33 rooms in all, with over 800 tatami mats, and in keeping with the rigid ranking of Tokugawa society there is a strict hierarchy. The first building was for reception of imperial messengers and the second for reception of feudal lords by shogunate ministers. The third was for meetings of the shogun with the so-called

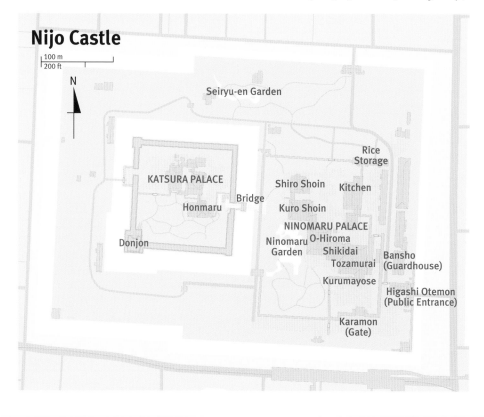

Nijo Castle

100 m
200 ft

N

Seiryu-en Garden

KATSURA PALACE

Rice Storage

Shiro Shoin   Kitchen

Bridge

Honmaru

Kuro Shoin

NINOMARU PALACE

Donjon

Ninomaru O-Hiroma
Garden   Shikidai

Tozamurai

Bansho (Guardhouse)

Kurumayose

Higashi Otemon (Public Entrance)

Karamon (Gate)

To the southwest of Ninomaru Palace lies a garden attributed to the primary landscape architect of early Tokugawa times, Kobori Enshu. A three-tiered waterfall feeds a pond that has a central Horai Island (Chinese symbol of Eternal Happiness), together with Crane and Turtle Islands representing good luck. The starkness of the rock arrangements lends the garden a rugged feeling, in keeping with the military might of the shogunate. According to tradition, Iemitsu did not want anything to remind him of life's transience, so there were originally no deciduous trees or plants, which would have heightened the effect.

The route back to the entrance leads past the Honmaru, an 1847 building from the Imperial Palace grounds donated by Prince Katsura. The Seiryu-en is a modern garden built by the city in 1965 for official events, with two teahouses and over 1,000 stones. Each cherry blossom season there is a special evening illumination, while in early June and November tea masters perform ceremonies for the public. A castle that was built to satisfy a shogun now serves the pleasure of the people.

KINKAKU-JI

THE FAMOUS TEMPLE OF THE GOLDEN PAVILION

**KINKAKU-JI
AT A GLANCE**

FEATURES Zen temple with pavilion and pond garden. Formal name Rokuon-ji (Deer Garden Temple).

ACCESS From Kyoto JR stn, bus 101/205 (40–50 mins) to Kinkakuji-michi bus stop, then 5 mins walk or subway line to Kitaoji stn and 10 mins taxi ride.

PRACTICALITIES 9.00–17.00. Y400. Temple tel. (075) 461-0013. Allow about 1 hour to visit.

DATELINE
1397—Founded by Ashikaga Yoshimitsu
1477—Golden Pavilion survives Onin War
1950—Pavilion burnt down
1955—Recreation completed

OPPOSITE The first floor of the Golden Pavilion comprises a reception area in the style of palace architecture. The second floor, for meetings, is in the samurai house style, while the third is in the Zen style with bell-shaped windows.

BELOW Kinkaku-ji's pond garden, originally filled with lotus plants, was intended to evoke a Buddhist paradise on the other side of the watery divide.

Kinkaku-ji is one of Japan's iconic images, and the silhouette of its golden pavilion is famous the world over. Many are surprised to learn that it is part of a functioning Zen temple, though not those familiar with Mishima's *Temple of the Golden Pavilion* (1956). The novel is based on a real-life incident when a novice monk burnt down the pavilion, and the present building is a painstaking reconstruction, completed in 1955. Now it is a must-see tourist sight whose radiant beauty is reflected in the pond in front of it.

The temple's origins lie with a powerful shogun, Ashikaga Yoshimitsu (1358–1408), the third of his family to hold power. He took early retirement in order to pursue the arts, and in 1397 transformed a villa on the northern hills into an expansive estate which included a palace and the Golden Pavilion. Under his patronage, artists flourished, and the so-called Kitayama (Northern Hills)

Culture developed in which potters, swordsmiths and other craftsmen produced goods of superlative quality (Noh was also first created at this time).

At his death, Yoshimitsu willed that the estate be turned into a Zen temple, but during the Onin War (1467–77) it was almost entirely wiped out—all except the Golden Pavilion. The three-storey structure is unusual in combining three distinct styles into a harmonious whole. The first floor is in the aristocratic style of the Heian Period, known as *shinden-zukuri*, and has a viewing area with verandas, unpainted wood and white plaster. When its shutters are opened, the room displays statues of Buddha and of Yoshimitsu, faintly visible from across the pond.

The second floor and third floors, intended to be more religious in orientation, reflect samurai and Zen styles. On the second floor is a Buddha Hall and shrine to Kannon, while on the third

floor, gilded on the inside as well as the outside, are housed relics of the Buddha.

In contrast to the plain wood of the first floor, the upper floors are lacquered and covered in gold leaf, the golden glow of which was thought to be spiritually purifying. (The effect was intensified by a 1984 restoration in which thicker gold leaf was added.)

The shingled roof of the building has a pyramid form, at the top of which is a bronze phoenix, appropriately for a building now risen from the flames.

The original statue of the bird survived, since it was away being repaired during the conflagration. The reflection of the building in the Mirror Pond conveys a sense of unreality, as if standing in another world, and the overall beauty of the scene is intended to suggest the Buddhist paradise.

The Muromachi Period (1333–1573) was a high point for Japanese garden design, and this is a classic example of the dynamic stroll garden, in which different perspectives open up as the visitor moves

TOP The third floor of the pavilion, with its views of nearby Mt Kinugasa, offered space for tea drinking and meditative contemplation. It once held statues of Amida and twenty-five bodhisattvas.

ABOVE Within the temple grounds is a pond whose small pagoda is dedicated to the White Dragon controlling the water supply.

around. The 'borrowed scenery' of Mt Kinugasa is used to extend the dimensional depth of the scene, and there are carefully placed focal points. At the back of the pavilion is a dock for a small boat, on which guests would once have been entertained by a leisurely tour as the host pointed out places of beauty or references to scenes from literature. There are ten small islands in all, the largest of which represents Japan. Four stones in a straight line near the pavilion suggest sailboats anchored on their way to the Isle of Eternal Life in Chinese mythology.

From the pond, the route leads visitors past the former living quarters of the head priest, not open to the public, and past the Anmintaku Pond where coins are tossed towards the statues for good luck. The Sekkatei Teahouse, added during the Edo Period, contains a celebrated pillar made from the nandin tree. Outside the exit of the compound is a temple hall housing a Fudo-myo statue, supposedly carved by the legendary Kukai, as well

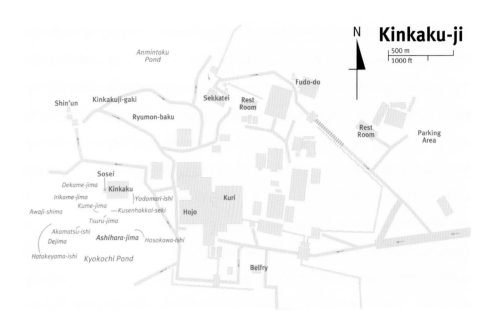

as places to enjoy whipped green tea (*matcha*). It makes a fitting way to round off a visit to this glittering gem of Japanese aesthetics, allowing one to reflect on the beauty within and the terrible ordeal that it has overcome.

BELOW Winter snow sets off the lacquered gold leaf of the pavilion's upper storeys, which stand in contrast to the plain wood of the first floor.

RYOAN-JI

JAPAN'S MOST RENOWNED ZEN ROCK GARDEN

FEATURES A Zen temple with dry landscape and pond gardens.

ACCESS From JR Kyoto stn, bus 101 or 205 (40 mins) or 20 mins walk from Kinkaku-ji.

PRACTICALITIES 8.00–17.00 (8.30–16.30 Dec–Feb). Y500. Temple tel. (075) 463-2216. Allow around 90 mins. Best to visit early morning or late afternoon.

DATELINE
1450—Founded as a private estate
1473—Conversion to a Zen temple
late 1400s—Creation of rock garden
1800—Temple rebuilt after fire

Ryoan-ji is synonymous with its rock garden although there's more than just that. It started life as an aristocratic estate with a large pond set beneath the northern hills. Later, the estate was converted into a Zen temple, and the rock garden was added around 1500, possibly by master designer Soami. Fire laid waste to the temple in 1797, following which it took its present form.

The route leads straight to the Hojo Hall (Abbot's Quarters), the veranda of which overlooks the famous rock garden. It contains nothing but white gravel and fifteen rocks, bordered by a yellowish clay wall. Various theories have been put forward to explain it: mountain peaks protruding from cloud, islands in a cosmic ocean, a Chinese riddle about tiger cubs.

The contrasting shapes of the rocks suggest yin–yang significance, while the groupings of seven, five and three are important numbers for Taoism. The key

RIGHT Ryoan-ji's water basin, donated in the seventeenth century, is shaped as a coin but bears an inscription that implies learning should be for its own sake, not for profit.

FAR RIGHT Visitors sit in contemplation of the temple's famous rock garden, with their backs to the Hojo Hall Abbot's Quarters. Intriguingly, not all the fifteen rocks can be seen at one time.

OPPOSITE TOP It's thought the rock garden was originally open-sided, and that the earthen wall made of clay boiled in oil was a later addition.

factor, however, could be that not all fifteen rocks can be seen at once. The fifteenth day in the lunar calendar signifies completion, with the implication being that 'the complete picture' can never be seen.

Inside the Hojo Hall is a set of six rooms with sliding screen (*fusuma*) paintings, and at the rear is a replica of the temple's famous water basin in which the central square represents the kanji for 'mouth'. The slogan it bears can be read to mean that learning should be for its own sake. At the same time, the water has a symbolic purpose, for it purifies the soul as well as washing the hands, and the overall effect is of a witty statement against materialism.

On the way back to the entrance, the pathway leads through moss-covered grounds and around the large pond with its hilly backdrop. Because of the popularity of the rock garden, there is little peace there for contemplation, but here in the spacious surrounds there comes a chance to pause for thought. Just fifteen rocks—but what a powerful impact!

ABOVE The sand base of the garden is raked daily in a set pattern. The only greenery in the garden is the moss around the base of the stones.

BELOW From the rock garden a path leads through a wooded area with an attractive moss ground covering.

OPPOSITE ABOVE Steps lead up to the Priests' Quarters, where a corridor leads off to the rock garden and the adjacent Abbot's Quarters.

OPPOSITE BELOW The temple's pond garden was created in the twelfth century and has two islands, on one of which is a small Benten shrine where one can pray for good fortune.

GINKAKU-JI

THE SERENE TEMPLE OF THE SILVER PAVILION

GINKAKU-JI AT A GLANCE

FEATURES A Rinzai Zen temple (formal name Jisho-ji) with Silver Pavilion, Hondo (Main Hall), Togudo Hall, dry landscape garden and pond garden.

ACCESS From Kyoto JR stn, bus no. 5, 17 or 100 to Ginkaku-ji mae (40 mins) or 10 mins by taxi from Shimogamo Shrine. Alternatively, walk along Philosopher's Walk from Nanzen-ji (30–40 mins).

PRACTICALITIES 8.30–17.00 (9.00–16.30 Dec–Feb). Y500. Temple tel. (075) 771-5725. Allow about 1 hour to visit.

DATELINE
1460—Work begins on an estate
1480—Work resumes after Onin War
1490—Conversion to Zen temple

The Silver Pavilion stands in Kyoto's northeast and was built by the grandson of the founder of the Golden Pavilion in the northwest. Erected almost a century later, it was intended to be a counterpart to its more famous predecessor. Both pavilions were originally part of large retirement estates. Both were converted to Zen temples following the death of the founder, and both were associated with artistic movements. But whereas one glistens with gold leaf, the other is strangely silver-less. Some think it all the finer for being so.

Unlike his grandfather, Ashikaga Yoshimasa (1436–90) did not distinguish himself as shogun, for the arts were more to his taste than politics. While the country crumbled around him, giving rise to the Onin War (1467–77) which destroyed most of Kyoto, Yoshimasa made plans for his retirement. The enormous estate he created (30 times its present size) contained a dozen pavilions for leisure pursuits such as moon viewing

and flower arrangement. The Higashi-yama (Eastern Hills) Culture that developed produced excellence in a number of fields, including poetry, garden design, architecture and the tea ceremony.

Of Yoshimasa's original estate, only two buildings have survived: the Silver Pavilion and the Togudo Hall. Like its predecessor, the two-storey pavilion mixes different styles in its architecture, with the residential style of the first floor set against the Zen style of the second. The roof is covered with overlapping shingles made of Japanese cypress, each of which is fixed in place with a bamboo nail. The route through the garden is designed so that after an initial glimpse of the pavilion, visitors are steered to a distant view from a hillside before being shown the building close up.

It is said that Yoshimasa's plan to add silver foil to the building was never implemented for lack of funds, but there may have been another factor. The retired shogun was an admirer of the poetic and spiritual qualities of the moon, which rose from behind the 'Moon Awaiting Hill' to spill its light on the lacquered exterior of the pavilion. The silvery light would have been intensified by the light reflected from the pond before it, and perhaps Yoshimasa decided this was sufficient. Ironically, given its name, the bare wood building is now hailed as an example of restraint and rustic sensibility.

The temple's striking dry landscape garden features the immaculately raked Sea of Silvery Sand. Raised above ground level, it is shaped after the famous West

RIGHT A bell-shaped window, typical of Zen architecture, looks onto the immaculately raked Sea of Silvery Sand.

OPPOSITE The Silver Pavilion and Mirror Pond survived from Ashikaga Yoshimasa's original estate, which had twelve buildings for the pursuit of artistic refinement. The garden is laid out so as to suggest famous literary scenes or beauty spots as one walks around.

ABOVE The Mirror Pond has Crane and Turtle Islands, symbolising good fortune. The pavilion was used for moon viewing, and in the garden is a Rock of Ecstatic Contemplation.

RIGHT Beyond the Sea of Silvery Sand stands the enigmatic Moon Viewing Platform (Kogetsudai). Some see it as a reference to Mt Fuji, while others believe it originated as a reserve supply of sand.

Lake in China and designed so as to appear to ripple in the moonlight. Next to it stands an enigmatic mound, said variously to represent a Chinese mountain or Mt Fuji. It was a later feature, which adds a dynamic yin–yang element to the horizontal flow of the 'sea'.

The Hondo (Main Hall), reconstructed in 2005, has seventeenth-century *fusuma* (sliding screen) paintings by the likes of Buson, and beyond this stands the Togudo Hall. Both buildings are only open in spring and autumn. The latter was Yoshimasa's private residential quarters, from the veranda of which he could view the pond garden. Built in 1486, it houses a chapel and study room with facility for the tea ceremony, the first known dedicated space. With its paper window, alcove and staggered shelving, the 4.5 tatami mat room is the oldest example of the *shoin-zukuri* style. Here is the prototype of what is today considered the standard Japanese room.

The beautiful pond garden, thought to be by master designer Soami, is laid out so as to provide fresh perspectives as the visitor moves around. There are seven small stone bridges and a miniature 'waterfall', while references to Japanese and Chinese literary scenes are skilfully woven into the garden features. The rocks were donated by Ashikaga supporters from all over Japan, and such is their special nature that each bears its own name and has its own recorded history.

The pathway leads the visitor up the nearby slope to a spring that feeds the pond below, and from where Yoshimasa drew water for his tea ceremonies. There are

vantage points over the temple grounds and the city beyond, and on the way down the route passes by a bamboo grove and a variety of moss. It's said that the value of a Japanese garden lies in the ability to suggest distance within a restricted space, and here within the compact grounds of Ginkaku-ji is a pathway that leads deep into the alluring world of Japanese aesthetics.

ABOVE The Silver Pavilion faces east towards the rising moon and away from the city in the river basin. Here was a wooded retreat for the aesthetes of Yoshimasa's circle, who wrote poems about the moon's transcendent beauty.

BELOW The garden path leads up an adjacent hill to offer fine views over the city and temple grounds. Visible here are the Sea of Silvery Sand, the Hondo (Main Hall) and the thatched roof of the Togudo Hall.

ENRYAKU-JI

A MONASTIC TEMPLE COMPLEX HIGH ATOP SACRED MOUNT HIEI

ENRYAKU-JI AT A GLANCE

FEATURES Tendai head temple with 3 precincts: To-to (Eastern Pagoda), Sai-to (Western Pagoda) and Yokawa.

ACCESS From Kyoto JR stn, bus no. 51 (I hr) or take the JR Kosei line to Hieizan-Sakamoto (14 mins), then bus (5 mins) and cable car (10 mins). Alternatively, go to Demachiyanagi and take the Eizan line to Yase stn, then cable car and ropeway (35 mins).

PRACTICALITIES 8.30–16.30 (March–Nov); 9.00–16.00 (Dec)/16.30 (Jan–Feb). Y550 entrance fee to all precincts (plus Y450 for museum). Shuttle buses between sites (one-day pass Y800). Temple tel. (077) 578-0001. Allow 1 whole day to see everything.

DATELINE
785—Saicho sets up hut on Mt Hiei
824—First use of the name Enryaku-ji
1571—Mountain razed by Nobunaga
1595—Restoration initiated

Enryaku-ji is often referred to as Hiei, the mountain on which it resides. Following the establishment of Heian-kyo in 794, the temple served as protector of the capital since it guarded the vulnerable northeast corner, known as Devil's Gate, through which evil spirits were thought to enter. At one point it was amongst the largest mountain monasteries in the world, and as a learning center it nurtured the great names of Japanese Buddhism: Honen (founder of the Pure Land sect), Shinran (True Pure Land), Eisai (Rinzai Zen), Dogen (Soto Zen), Nichiren (Nichiren/Soka Gakkai) and Ippen (Ji sect).

The temple originated with a monk called Saicho (767–822), who as a youth built a worship-hut on Mt Hiei. In 804 he joined an imperial mission to China where he studied at Mt Tiantai (Tendai in

RIGHT The Bell of Good Fortune hangs near the Great Lecture Hall. Visitors can pay Y50 to ring it and make a wish.

FAR RIGHT The Western Precinct (Sai-to) has a pair of symmetrical buildings for spiritual training. One serves for walking meditation, the other for reflection on the Lotus Sutra.

OPPOSITE TOP The Chu-do (Central Hall) of the Yokawa Precinct was rebuilt in 1971 after being struck by lightning. The original building was first erected in the ninth century.

ABOVE The Amida Hall in the Eastern Precinct (To-to), rebuilt in 1937, is connected by an overhead passageway to a two-storey pagoda and has a charnel house behind it.

LEFT There are several Shinto shrines at Enryaku-ji although it is a Buddhist temple, as the Tendai sect recognises the existence of *kami* (divine spirits).

Japanese). On his return, he established a monastery for the new teaching, and a year after he died the sect won the much prized right of ordination. It marked an important shift away from the powerful Nara sects which had previously held a monopoly.

Tendai's form of Buddhism is pragmatic, privileges the Heart Sutra and incorporates belief in Amida with Zen meditation. Esoteric techniques are practised along with mountain austerities. The training can be severe, with long hours of spiritual discipline in the bitter mountain cold. The ultimate challenge is undertaken by *ajari*, whose twelve-year course involves circling the mountain before dawn and fasting for ten days without sleep or water.

Two hundred years after Saicho, the monastery had grown into a sprawling complex that covered the mountain and whose will was enforced by warrior-monks. It led to clashes with the state, and on occasion the militant monks would descend *en masse* to the capital below to lend force to their argument. So powerful did the temple become that in

1571 the unifier of Japan, Oda Nobunaga, ordered his troops to destroy it. The mountain was systematically razed, and in the process some 3,000 buildings were burnt and 25,000 people, including women and children, perished. It's said

that Kyoto's sky was black for three days and that the waters of Lake Biwa turned warm.

The temple revived, though never as big as before, and today it exudes an air of ancient traditions. Picture boards line the

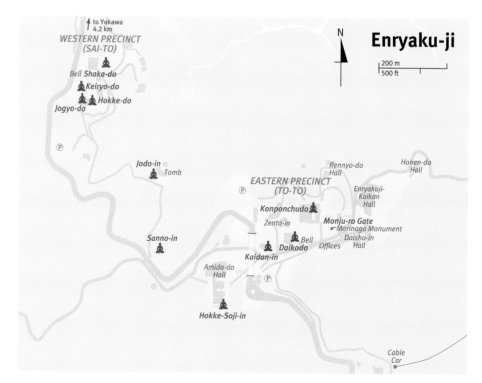

RIGHT TOP The rebuilt Kaidan-in (Ordination Hall) is held in great esteem, for its predecessor marked the recognition of Tendai as an independent sect.

RIGHT MIDDLE The Daikodo (Great Lecture Hall) contains portraits of the great teachers of the past, who sustained the temple's reputation for scholarship.

RIGHT BOTTOM The main building of the Western Precinct (Sai-to) is the huge Shakado, which was moved here in 1595 from the Mii-dera Temple at Lake Biwa.

pathways depicting biographical scenes from the past, and the temple's main building, Konponchudo, stands on the site of Saicho's hut. Reconstructed in 1642, it has a unique design by which worshippers look down from a raised platform on a half-lit area in which priests carry out their rituals. From out of the gloom glimmer the gold-leaf forms of Buddhist deities, and before the central altar are 'eternal flames' kept burning since the time of Saicho.

Other buildings in the To-to precinct include the Ordination Hall (Kaidan-in), which commemorates the winning of imperial recognition in 823, and the Great Lecture Hall, decorated with portraits of former teachers. A pleasant twenty-five minute walk away lies another set of buildings, known as Sai-to. The path leads through woods, and on the way one passes Saicho's mausoleum, complete with Worship Hall, and a pair of buildings reserved for spiritual exercises such as walking meditation. The precinct's main building is the immense Shakado, relocated here in 1595, which proved the first step in the revival of the temple after its destruction by Nobunaga.

Some 2.5 miles (4 km) to the north is Yokawa, another group of buildings set in the woods. Its Central Hall (Chuo-do) stands on a steep slope supported by pillars, and was reconstructed in 1971 after being destroyed by lightning. Joko-in is where the influential Nichiren lived for twelve years, and the Eshin-do is named after a twelfth-century monk instrumental in the spread of Pure Land belief. Though Yokowa is the least visited precinct, the wealth of historical association even here attests to the fact that this is a very special mountain—'the mother mountain of Japanese Buddhism'.

TO-JI

JAPAN'S LARGEST PAGODA AND THE SYMBOL OF KYOTO

OPPOSITE TOP LEFT The Great South Gate (Nandaimon) faces onto the Kondo (Main Hall) and was moved here in 1894. It was formerly the West Gate of Sanjusangendo.

OPPOSITE TOP RIGHT A shrine guards the Buddhist pagoda, for Kukai, who refounded To-ji, recognised native *kami* as guardians of the spirit of place.

OPPOSITE BOTTOM To-ji's famous pagoda has burnt down five times in its history and the present structure dates from 1644. On its ground floor are statues of Four Buddhas and on the walls paintings of Eight Great Bodhisattvas.

Toji's pagoda, the largest in Japan, has become a symbol of Kyoto although there is more to the temple than that. It houses one of the most stunning collections of statuary as well as being a lively working institution and hosting popular monthly markets. Although the original buildings have been lost, the original layout remains in place. The present compound, with its 24 acres (10 hectares), is just a quarter of the size it once was, and though visitors can enter the grounds for free, they have to pay to enter the inner precinct with its prized possessions.

When Emperor Kammu set up a new capital in 794, he allowed for the construction of two guardian temples on either side of the Rashomon entrance gate: To-ji (East Temple) and the now defunct Sai-ji (West Temple). In 823, Kammu's son, Emperor Saga, entrusted To-ji to the eminent priest Kukai, who enlarged and transformed it into a seminary for the teaching he had introduced from China. An esoteric form of Buddhism, Shingon mixes metaphysics with 'magical' rituals in which mudra (hand gestures) play an important part.

The chief structures are set around a pond garden in which the eye is drawn to the pagoda in the southeast corner. First erected in 826, it was destroyed four times by lightning and the present building dates back to 1644. Inside (only occasionally open for viewing) are four statues of different Buddhas arranged around the central square-shaped pillar. At 179 feet (55 meters) high, the pagoda towered over the city's wooden buildings before the advent of high-rises post-war.

ABOVE A large statue of Kukai (also known as Kobo Daishi, his posthumous name) stands near the Great South Gate. He remains a revered figure, not only for his teaching but for his legacy of good works.

LEFT To-ji stands within a walled compound of 24 acres (10 hectares), which is a quarter of its former size. Visitors can enter the compound for free but have to pay to visit the pond garden and main buildings.

The Main Hall (Kondo), reconstructed in 1603, is notable for its south-facing double-roof design, with the raised central part offsetting the regularity of the rest. The central figure of worship is a 9.6 foot (2.9 meter) wooden statue of Yakushi Nyorai set against a huge aureole and with Twelve Heavenly Generals supporting the pedestal. To either side stand attendants, Nikko (sun deity) and Gakko (moon), and the ensemble exudes a sense of compassion towards those who are suffering.

The adjacent Kodo (Lecture Hall), reconstructed in 1491, houses a stunning collection of 21 statues used for instructional purposes. The figures are arranged in the form of a mandala, at the center of which is the prime mover of the universe, Dainichi Nyorai. Around the central deity are arranged buddhas, boddhisattvas, attendants and guardians. The awesome size of the statues, the serene expressions of the enlightened and the fearsome poses of their protectors combine to make this one of Kyoto's finest spectacles.

Outside the inner precinct are several items of interest. The former refectory is given over to exhibitions, and the

Homotsukan museum (only open in spring and autumn) has some fine Buddhist statuary as well as calligraphy by Kukai (known posthumously as Kobo Daishi). The Shingon founder remains an inspirational presence, remembered fondly for his good works and the opportunity for salvation he taught. He not only opened a school for the poor but he produced the first ever Japanese dictionary to promote literacy.

A statue of Kukai stands inside the Great South Gate and a memorial hall, called Miedo (or Taishido), stands on the site of his residence. The hall houses a statue of him made in 1223, in front of which a six o'clock service is held every morning. The walled compound is open to the public but the hall itself is only available for viewing on the 21st of the month when a monthly market called Kobo-san takes place (in reference to Kukai's posthumous name).

One of the oldest and largest markets in Japan, Kobo-san began some 700 years ago when merchants saw an opportunity to sell green tea to the crowds that gathered in Kukai's memory. Only licensed traders can have stalls and some have been coming for generations to sell such items as antiques, plants, food, crafts and Japanese miscellanea. Many of the vendors—and buyers—will make time to pay their respects to Kobo Daishi in the nearby memorial hall, proving that piety and profit co-exist as happily now as they did hundreds of years ago.

BELOW The Kodo (Lecture Hall) is the temple's most important building for it contains the essence of Kukai's teachings in the form of 21 statues arranged as a three-dimensional mandala.

BOTTOM Toji is particularly popular at cherry blossom time when the grounds are illuminated. It is crowded also on the 21st of every month for the Kobo-san flea market of Japan crafts.

BYODO-IN

THE ELEGANT PHOENIX HALL TEMPLE TO AMIDA'S PURE LAND

**BYODO-IN
AT A GLANCE**

FEATURES A joint Jodo-Tendai temple with Phoenix Hall, pond garden and museum.

ACCESS From Kyoto JR stn, train to Uji JR (17 mins), then 15 mins walk. Alternatively, Keihan line to Uji stn, then 10 mins walk.

PRACTICALITIES 8.30–17.30. Y600 (includes museum). Temple tel. (0774) 21-2861. Allow about 90 mins.

FOUNDATION 1052, by Fujiwara no Yorimichi

The Phoenix Hall of Byodo-in has been called 'the most beautiful building in Japan' and its image is stamped on the back of Y10 coins. It stands before a lotus pond, and from its central hall extend two 'wings' in the form of long, curving corridors. These lend the building the appearance of a bird taking flight, and for the historian George Sansom it has 'such an airy grace that it seems to be rising to escape from earthly sorrows'.

The temple lies south of Kyoto, along a stretch of river used by Heian nobles for country retreats. One estate belonged to Fujiwara no Michinaga, the most powerful man of his day, and after his death it was turned into a temple by his son. It coincided with the first year in 'the last stage in the decline of Buddhism' (a theory known as *mappo*). Against such a background, there arose a strong belief in one particular Buddha called Amida, who had promised to accept into his Pure Land anyone who entrusted themselves to him.

The temple originally had some thirty buildings but miraculously only the

Phoenix Hall has survived. It is best seen from across the pond, looking towards the west (the direction of Amida's Pure Land). Inside the hall is a seated gold-leaf Amida, 8 feet (2.5 meters) tall, surrounded by celestial figures. The interior was kept purposefully dark so that the candle-lit figures would appear to be a heavenly vision floating on the far side of the shimmering water.

Byodo-in became the model for other Pure Land gardens (there were once 100 Amida halls around Kyoto), and in the temple museum is an informative display

TOP A phoenix stands on the roof in reference to the building's name, adopted because of its resemblance to the mythical bird. The original name was the Amida Hall.

ABOVE The perfect symmetry and gracefulness of the design has won many admirers. Details of the construction and interior can be found in the temple's Treasury.

LEFT The two wings of the Phoenix Hall reach out like the arms of Amida, a huge statue of whom is housed in the central structure. Although the hall appears to have two storeys, in fact there is only one in order to contain the almost 10-foot (3-meter)-high seated figure.

which includes a recreation of the original color scheme. It doesn't take much imagination to realise how radiant a jewel the temple would have been in an age of gathering gloom. Even now, after almost 1,000 years, the power of the Pure Land vision shines through in the exquisite beauty of the building.

UJIGAMI JINJA

JAPAN'S OLDEST SURVIVING SHINTO STRUCTURE

**UJIGAMI JINJA
AT A GLANCE**

FEATURES Shinto shrine with ancient Honden (Sanctuary), Haiden (Worship Hall), and Kiriharasui Spring.

ACCESS From Kyoto JR stn, train to JR Uji (17 mins) and walk 20 mins. Alternatively, the Keihan line goes to Uji stn, then 10 mins walk.

PRACTICALITIES 9.00–16.30. Free. Tel. (0774) 21-4634. English language leaflet for Y100. Allow 30 mins (best done in conjunction with Byodo-in). Uji Volunteer Guide Club (0774) 22-5063.

FOUNDATION Origins unclear, but possibly ninth or tenth century.

The small town of Uji to the south of Kyoto is famous for green tea and as a setting for the last part of *The Tale of Genji* (c. 1005). It is also home to two World Heritage Sites, one of which (Ujigami) is a protective shrine for the other (Byodo-in). Although the shrine is modest in appearance, it is of historic value because its Honden (Sanctuary) dates to around 1067, making it the oldest Shinto structure in Japan.

Until 1868 Ujigami was part of a larger complex that included its neighbor, Uji Shrine. The complex was thought to stand on the site of a villa belonging to Prince Uji Wakiiratsuko, the younger son of Emperor Ojin (c. 300). The prince was appointed heir by his father but became involved in a succession dispute with his elder brother (Emperor Nintoku) and drowned himself in the Uji River.

Ojin, Nintoku and Wakiiratsuko were all enshrined as *kami*, and when Byodo-in was established, Ujigami Jinja was made its guardian. Unusually, the Honden comprises three adjacent shrines within an outer structure, whose sweeping cypress bark roof covering the entrance on the long side is typical of the *nagare-zukuri* shrine style. By contrast, the Haiden (Worship Hall) is in the aristocratic residential style (*shinden-zukuri*),

RIGHT ABOVE The *torii* gate of Ujigami Shrine, festooned with *shimenawa* rice rope and *shide* paper streamers, marks a symbolic entrance into sacred space.

RIGHT BELOW The Honden at New Year remains a popular place for paying respects nearly 1,000 years after being built. Its sweeping roof covering the entrance, typical of shrine architecture, is in the *nagare-zukuri* style.

precinct, is a wooded slope and the shrine sees itself as 'a buffer zone between untamed wilderness and residential areas'. Here, in this liminal space, the ancient shrine buildings have for almost 1,000 years served the community for animistic worship and the honoring of imperial ancestors.

ABOVE The Worship Hall, built in the Kamakura Period, has claims to be among the oldest of its type. Unlike the Honden where the *kami* reside, the Worship Hall is for human use and built in the residential style of Heian palaces.

LEFT Kiriharasui is the only functioning spring to remain from Uji's Seven Famous Waters.

BELOW Ikebana arrangements decorate the Worship Hall at New Year. The shutters that open upwards and outwards are typical of the Heian residential style.

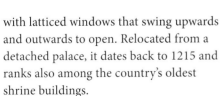

with latticed windows that swing upwards and outwards to open. Relocated from a detached palace, it dates back to 1215 and ranks also among the country's oldest shrine buildings.

Pure water was important to a town famed for its tea, and Uji once boasted Seven Famous Springs. Only Kiriharasui at Ujigami remains. The others no longer function. Beyond it, at the back of the

NISHI HONGAN-JI

THE TEMPLE OF THE PRIMAL VOW

FEATURES A head temple of Jodo Shinshu (True Pure Land Sect) with Amida-do (Amida Hall), Goeido (Founder's Hall) and Karamon Gate. [Also guided tour available of Shoin rooms, Noh stage and Hiunkaku (Pavilion of the Floating Clouds)].

ACCESS From Kyoto JR stn, 10 mins walk northwest.

PRACTICALITIES 5.30–17.30/18.00 (May–Aug), 6.00–17.00 (Nov–Feb). Entrance free. Tel. (075) 371-5181. Allow up to 1 hour. Guided tour in Japanese 14.30–15.30 (apply in advance).

FOUNDATION 1591, on land provided by Hideyoshi. (Antecedents go back to a mausoleum for Shinran in Yamashina in 1272.)

Nishi Hongan-ji is one of a pair of temples to the north of Kyoto's railway station. There was originally one Hongan-ji temple, but in 1602 it split into West (Nishi) and East (Higashi) following a dispute over succession. There is no doctrinal difference, but each temple heads its own faction of Jodo Shinshu (True Pure Land sect) which follows the teaching of Shinran (1173–1263). His philosophy was based on the notion that salvation could be obtained through a Buddha called Amida ('Hongan-ji' means Temple of the Primal Vow in reference to the deity's promise to save his followers).

The temple compound is dominated by two huge wooden buildings. The Amida Hall, built in 1760, has 132 pillars and a capacity of 1,500. Along with the central image of Amida, it has portraits of Pure

BELOW The lavishly decorated Karamon (Chinese-style gate) is also known as the Higurashimon (Gate of Dusk) because one can look at it all day without tiring.

ABOVE Schoolchildren are guided past the Amida Hall, dating from 1760, which stands next to the even larger Founder's Hall to the south.

LEFT The double-roofed Kyodo (Sutra Library), built in 1678, contains a complete set of Buddhist scriptures. Within the temple precinct can also be found a Bell Tower and a Drum Tower.

BELOW A connecting corridor runs between the two large temple halls, enabling visitors to move from one to the other without footwear.

Land prophets from India, China and Japan. The Founder's Hall, or Goeido, is an even larger building, with 227 pillars and a capacity of 3,000. The central image of worship is a statue of Shinran, coated in lacquer mixed with his cremated ashes (Hongan-ji, in fact, started as a mausoleum temple).

To the south of the Goeido stands an elaborate Karamon Gate with carvings of Chinese moral tales and auspicious motifs. Relocated from Fushimi Castle, it is typical of the flamboyant artistic style of the Momoyama Period (1575–1615). The temple houses many other items from the period, some of which can be seen on a guided tour. These include superlative room paintings, Japan's largest outdoor Noh stage and an ingenious garden created in the dry landscape style.

The tour of Nishi Hongan-ji ends with the Pavilion of the Floating Clouds, a three-storey building ranked alongside its Golden and Silver counterparts. It turns out that behind the somber façade of the huge temple halls lies an unexpected and unseen world—one of Momoyama magnificence.

DAIGO-JI

AN IMPERIAL MOUNTAIN RETREAT

**DAIGO-JI
AT A GLANCE**

FEATURES Shingon temple in 2 areas.
Lower Daigo (Shimo Daigo) includes
Sambo-in, Main Hall, pagoda, Benten Pond
and museum. Upper Daigo (Kami Daigo) lies
2.5 miles (4 km) uphill and marks the temple's
origins. It includes the Yakushido Hall.

ACCESS From Kyoto stn, subway to Daigo
stn changing at Oike (30 mins) and then
15 mins walk or shuttle bus. Alternatively,
JR train to Yamashina (5 mins) or Rokujizo
(11 mins), then Keihan bus no. 22 to
Daigo-Sanboin-mae (15 mins).

PRACTICALITIES 9.00–17.00/16.00
(Dec–Jan). Combinatory tickets Y1000/1500.
Kami Daigo Y600. Temple tel. (075) 571-0002;
fax (075) 571-0101. English website: www.
daigoji.or.jp. Allow 2 hours for Shimo Daigo.
The walk to Upper Daigo takes 1 hour uphill.

EVENTS
Feb 23—Godaraiki (fire and rice cake lifting)
April 2nd Sun—Cherry blossom procession
June 7—Mountain ascetics leave for Mt
    Omine

FOUNDATION 874, by the monk Shobo (also
known as Rigen Daishi).

Within its wooded grounds Daigo-ji
houses 18 National Treasures, the most
famous of which is the Sambo-in subtemple with its magnificent garden.
In addition, there is an outstanding
museum, a picturesque pond and Kyoto's
oldest standing structure, a pagoda
from 951. Set on a hillside, the temple
is popular during the time of cherry
blossom and autumn colors. Most
visitors stay in Lower Daigo, yet here,
just 20 minutes from downtown, is a
rare opportunity to hike in the hills.

The temple's origins concern the location
of a spring revealed in a vision, and the
building erected there became the basis
of Upper Daigo. Imperial patronage led,
in 926, to development at the base of the
hill. Although the complex was destroyed
on several occasions, the decaying temple
was restored by the sixteenth-century ruler
Toyotomi Hideyoshi.

Under Hideyoshi's patronage, Sambo-in
was rebuilt with gorgeous paintings, tea
rooms, a Noh stage and a garden containing over 700 boulders brought from all

RIGHT The Benten Pond, with its gracefully arched
bridge and vermilion shrine, is particularly popular with
photographers, both during the cherry blossom period
and for the maple leaves in autumn.

OPPOSITE TOP The Daigo-ji pagoda is Kyoto's oldest
standing structure. Although it is not open to the public,
it houses some rare religious paintings thought to be
the earliest surviving examples of their type.

over Japan. It was used as a base for an extravagant cherry blossom event in 1598, when accompanied by 1,000 people Hideyoshi was carried up the hillside to admire the views, which on a clear day extend as far as Osaka.

Upper Daigo has a more austere feel. It is not only a center for mountain asceticism (Shugendo) but part of two major pilgrimages. Prominent amongst the buildings is the Yakushido, built in 1121, which houses an image from 907. On the way up the hill, visitors pass the original spring, housed now in a shrine to show its waters are for spiritual as well as physical nourishment. It was from here that flowed the inspiration for this remarkable hillside complex.

BELOW The Imperial Messenger's Gate at Sambo-in, only for ceremonial use, bears the imperial symbol of a 16-petal chrysanthemum alongside Hideyoshi's paulownia.

BOTTOM Daigo-ji has some 70 wooden structures in all. Most were destroyed in the Onin War (1467–77), but like this bell tower were subsequently rebuilt.

KAMIGAMO JINJA
ONE OF KYOTO'S OLDEST SHINTO SHRINES

**KAMIGAMO JINJA
AT A GLANCE**

FEATURES Shinto shrine with 34 structures in 170 acres (68 hectares).

ACCESS From Kyoto JR stn, subway to Kitayama stn (15 mins) and 15 mins walk or take bus no. 4 to the last stop (from Kyoto JR stn I hour) or from Shimogamo Shrine (30 mins).

PRACTICALITIES 8.00/8.30–16.00. Free. Tour and purification in English 9.30–10.00 (book in advance; Y500 donation). Shrine tel. (075) 781-0011; fax (075) 702-6618. Allow 60–90 mins.

FOUNDATION Unknown, though possibly sixth century; reconstructed 1628.

ABOVE The roof of the shrine's main gateway bears a crest of *aoi* leaves (loosely translated as hollyhock). During the annual Aoi Festival in May, participants wear the leaves as they were once thought to offer protection from disasters.

TOP A small arched bridge stands over one of the two streams running through the grounds. Behind it, the thatched roof entrance gate leads into the shrine's inner compound where, unusually, can be found both a Honden (Main Sanctuary) and a Gonden (Temporary Sanctuary).

Kamigamo claims to be Kyoto's oldest shrine although its origins are unclear. It is certainly Kyoto's greenest, thanks to spacious surroundings that give it the appearance of a park. It lies on the city's northern outskirts, upstream from its sister shrine, Shimogamo. The two shrines are associated with the Kamo clan, who settled in the area before the founding of the Heian-kyo capital, and Kamigamo enshrines a thunder deity called Kamo Wake-ikazuchi, who was grandson of the clan's founding father, who is worshipped at Shimogamo.

Following the establishment of Heian-kyo, the Kamo shrines became the beneficiary of imperial patronage, apparent in the influence of Buddhist temples. Kamigamo's inner compound has a magnificent multistorey red entrance gate fronted by a small curved bridge which stands over one of the two streams running through the grounds. The buildings are nearly all 1628 reconstructions of the Heian-era originals, although the Honden and Gonden sanctuaries, with their painted *komainu* (lion-dog) guardians, date from 1863. The Gonden is unique in being a permanent 'spare' sanctuary for the *kami*.

Like Shimogamo, the shrine is one of the few to follow an ancient tradition of renewal called *shikinen sengu*. This used to involve complete rebuilding every twenty-one years, but is now restricted to renewing and repairing. Another unusual feature is a pair of conical sand mounds, said to be yin–yang signifiers for the shrine's sacred Mt Ko, onto which the *kami* first descended.

Kamigamo hosts a number of annual events, including horse archery, children's

sumo and a Heian-style poetry competition. It is best known, however, for the Aoi Matsuri held every May, which originated around 544 to appease the local deity after bad weather had ruined crops. The modern version features a parade of over 500 participants in period costume, who accompany an imperial messenger to the Kamo shrines where he makes offerings and petitions. It's a fine example of the intangible cultural heritage Kamigamo maintains, along with its striking physical properties.

ABOVE Various interpretations have been put forward to explain the conical sand mounds in front of the Heiden (Offertory). Some say they are for purification purposes, while others see them as yin–yang signifiers of the shine's sacred hill.

RIGHT The horse archery event held every autumn, known as Kasagake, involves galloping at high speed while aiming at small targets. The display of medieval fighting skill makes good use of Kamigamo's wide open space.

SHIMOGAMO JINJA

AN ANCIENT CITY SHRINE SURROUNDED BY WOODLAND

**SHIMOGAMO JINJA
AT A GLANCE**

FEATURES Shinto shrine of 55 structures
set in 30 acres (12 hectares) of ancient
woodland (Tadasu no mori). The main
compound houses a dance stage, musician's
stage, Chinese zodiac shrines and purification
pond. An auxiliary shrine, Kawai Jinja, houses
a model of a famous literary hut.

ACCESS From JR Kyoto stn, city bus 205
or 4 (about 30 mins). Alternatively, from
Demachiyanagi on the Keihan line, 8 mins
walk.

PRACTICALITIES 6.30–17.00. Free. Shrine
tel. (075) 781-0010. Allow about 90 mins.

EVENTS
Jan 4—Kemari kickball display
May 3—Yabusame (horseback archery)
May 15—Aoi Festival parade

FOUNDATION Unknown, but possibly sixth
century.

**Shimogamo Shrine is part of a pair of
shrines** associated historically with the
Kamo clan, who settled in the area before
Kyoto was founded. Shimogamo is 'the
lower shrine' since it stands downstream
from Kamigamo ('the upper shrine'). It
enshrines clan founder Kamo Taketsu-
numi and his daughter Princess Tama-
yori, mother of the Kamigamo deity.
Following the establishment of Heian-kyo
in 794, the two Kamo shrines were made
guardians of the new capital and ranked
amongst the highest in the land. Buddhist
architectural elements are apparent.

Situated at the confluence of two rivers,
Shimogamo has claims to be Kyoto's
'power spot'. The layout dates to the early
eleventh century and consists of an outer
and inner compound fronted by a
two-storey gate. To the right stands the
Mitarashi pond, fed by a natural spring,
where purification rites are held. Within
the inner compound are sanctuaries for
the two *kami*, and there are small shrines

RIGHT Water was treasured by early Japanese as a vital
life-giving resource, and Shimogamo stands at the
intersection of the Takano and Kamo Rivers. The Mitarashi
Stream running through the east side of the shrine is
thought to carry sacred water.

also for the Chinese years of the zodiac, where worshippers pray to the deity governing their year of birth.

The shrine is noted for its ancient woodland, which is a remnant of the primeval forest that once covered Kyoto's river basin, and is mentioned in literary works such as *The Tale of Genji* (c. 1005). The deciduous trees and splashing streams give a sense of immersion in nature. There is a pavilion to take tea, and a subshrine called Kawai Jinja houses a model of the hut used by the thirteenth-century recluse Kamo no Chomei.

The shrine organises many annual events, the principal being the Aoi Festival (see pages 76–7). Among the preliminary activities is a demonstration of horse archery (Yabusame) re-enacting medieval riding skills. Other events include *kemari* 'football' at New Year, a firefly festival, foot purification in the shrine's sacred pond, and moon viewing in the autumn. In this way, surrounded by the ancient woods, the shrine continues the tradition of animism and ancestor worship which lie at the roots of Japanese culture.

TOP Participants in Heian-era clothing line up in the main compound prior to departing for Mt Mikage, where the shrine's *kami* is received and brought back to Shimogamo in readiness for the annual Aoi Festival.

ABOVE The Mitarashi Shrine stands at the spot where the sacred waters enter the shrine grounds. Purification rites take place here, including an annual leg protection festival when people wade barefoot through the water.

RIGHT Women in Heian-era costume at one of the events leading up to the Aoi Festival accompany the Saoi-dai. The young woman represents the unmarried imperial princess who was appointed to oversee rites at the two Kamo shrines from 812 to 1212.

TENRYU-JI

THE TEMPLE OF THE HEAVENLY DRAGON

**TENRYU-JI
AT A GLANCE**

FEATURES Rinzai Zen temple with Sogenchi pond garden. Also Sanmon Gate, Butsuden Hall, Hatto (Lecture Hall) and Hojo (Abbot's Quarters).

ACCESS From Kyoto JR stn, train to JR Saga Arashiyama (15 mins), then 10 mins walk or bus to Keifuku Arashiyama (time depends on traffic), then 5 mins walk.

PRACTICALITIES 8.30–17.30. Y500. Hatto Y500. Temple tel. (075) 881-1235; fax (075) 864-2424. Allow up to 90 mins.

FOUNDATION 1339, by the shogun Ashikaga Takauji.

BELOW At the temple entrance is a small rock garden, which exemplifies the ability of 'dry landscapes' to condense scenery into the smallest of spaces.

OPPOSITE ABOVE The garden pathway leads up the adjacent hillside, landscaped so as to provide views over the temple buildings below. Of the 150 subtemples that once existed, only 13 remain today.

OPPOSITE BELOW The Sogen Pond lies next to the Abbot's Quarters from where it is seen to best advantage. Groupings of rocks provide focal points and lead the eye towards the hills beyond.

Located near the popular resort of Arashiyama, Tenryu-ji boasts a garden of historical distinction designed by its first abbot, Muso Soseki (1275–1351). The temple was established by the shogun Ashikaga Takauji for the repose of Emperor Godaigo, whom he had betrayed. By way of propitiation, Takauji built a temple on the site of a villa in which the emperor had spent his childhood, and it soon became one of Kyoto's leading Zen institutions.

Over the centuries, the temple was razed by fire on eight different occasions, and nearly all the buildings are modern reconstructions. The oldest structure is the Chokushimon Gate, built in the flamboyant Momoyama style (1573–1615). In the center of the grounds stands the Lecture Hall (Hatto), a 1900 reconstruction with a central image of the historical Buddha (Shaka Nyorai) and a ceiling painting of a dragon amongst the clouds (Tenryu-ji means Temple of the Heavenly Dragon).

Unlike the buildings, the pond garden has survived from Soseki's original design. It is arranged in traditional style as a promenade or 'stroll' garden, with a circular walk around a nearby slope so that the waterfalls, stone bridges and rock islands can be admired from a variety of perspectives. But Soseki also introduced a new element into the garden—that of contemplative viewing. Rather than physically entering the garden, the onlooker enters visually. It marked a shift in aesthetic sensibility, influenced by the spread of Zen amongst the ruling samurai.

The garden is intended for viewing
from the Abbot's Quarters, and the focal
point is a group of vertical rocks reflected
in the water. Beyond them is the oldest
surviving example of a technique called
'borrowed scenery' (*shakkei*), whereby the
surrounding hills are carefully integrated
into the design. The overall effect is of a
three-dimensional work of art, representing a breakthrough that was to have a
profound influence on later creations.
(For another garden by Muso Soseki, see
Saiho-ji, pages 86–7.)

NINNA-JI

THE TEMPLE OF HEAVENLY BENEVOLENCE

FEATURES Shingon temple with Omuro Palace, cherry grove, Nio Gate, Main Hall (Kondo) and pagoda.

ACCESS From Kyoto JR stn, bus to Omuro Ninna-ji (40 mins). Alternatively, from Ryoan-ji, 10 mins walk.

PRACTICALITIES 9.00–17.00/16.00 (winter). Grounds free, Omuro Palace Y500. Temple tel. (075) 461-1155. Allow about 90 mins.

FOUNDATION 888, by Emperor Uda.

Ninna-ji has strong aristocratic connections, which derive from its founder, Emperor Uda. In 888, he supervised completion of a temple in the western foothills, and after retiring assumed the post of first abbot. For nearly 1,000 years (to 1869), Uda was succeeded in the post by an imperial prince, and the high status of the abbots is reflected in their residence (Omuro Palace) styled in the manner of an aristocrat's villa. It was reconstructed in 1915 following fire, and it is the highlight of a visit.

The palace has well-appointed buildings with connecting corridors, set around a walled garden. In the entrance hall stands a gorgeous ikebana display by the Omuro school, based at the temple. The main building consists of three large rooms with paintings by acclaimed modern artists, and from the veranda is a picturesque view of the pond garden with its teahouse and pagoda beyond. It's a quintessential Japanese scene.

Entrance to Ninna-ji is through an enormous Niomon Gate, serving as a reminder of how big the temple once was. It was destroyed in the Onin War (1467–77), and the present buildings such as the five-storey pagoda are mainly reconstructions from the 1630s. It was then that a grove of 200 late flowering

cherry trees was planted, for which the temple is now most famous.

Amongst the temple's other buildings is the Reihokan Museum, only open in spring and autumn, which has a fine collection of Buddhist artifacts. The Kondo (Main Hall) houses an Amida triad, and like the Miedo (Founder's Hall) was originally an imperial palace building. The latter honors Kukai, who started the Shingon sect, and through the back gate of the temple is a hillside with a miniature version of the 88 temple pilgrimage in Shikoku associated with him. For those with time, the two-hour walk leads to a different realm altogether,

away from courtly aesthetics and into the heart of nature.

OPPOSITE The garden of the Omuro Palace is best seen first from the raised area of the Remeiden altar, looking towards the former abbot's residence, from the veranda of which is the perfect spot for contemplative viewing.

ABOVE LEFT The five-storey pagoda, erected in 1637, dominates the temple grounds. Facing it is a grove of late flowering Omuro cherry trees for which Ninna-ji is justifiably famous.

ABOVE RIGHT Fire devastated the Omuro Palace in 1887, and the re-created rooms are decorated with some stunning paintings by modern artists.

BELOW LEFT The temple's Hondo (Main Hall) was moved here in 1676 from the Imperial Palace, where it had acted as Ceremonial Hall. It now houses an Amida triad with golden aureoles.

ABOVE The thatched Chokushimon (Imperial Messenger's Gate) in the entrance courtyard of the Omuro Palace is kept closed as it is only for ceremonial use.

BELOW At the entrance to the temple stands a large Sanmon Gate, inside which on the left-hand side a smaller entrance gate leads into the grounds of the Omuro Palace.

ABOVE A striking two-storey bell tower stands at the back of the temple grounds, next to a Founder's Hall and a Fudo-myo statue for pouring water over.

LEFT The huge Sanmon entrance gate, with its enormous Nio guardian figures, was rebuilt in the 1630s and ranks as one of the biggest in Japan.

BELOW The panoramic view of the Omuro Palace's pond garden, as seen from the veranda of the former abbot's residence, centers on the Hiro-tei Teahouse, behind which rises the five-storey pagoda in the temple compound beyond.

TOP The guardian shrine of Ninna-ji is the Kusho Myojin Jinja, which stands in its own grounds within the temple precinct.

ABOVE Like other Kyoto temples, Ninna-ji was destroyed in the Onin War (1467–77), which raged across the city. The present buildings date from its reconstruction in the 1630s.

SAIHO-JI
THE TEMPLE OF MOSS

**SAIHO-JI
AT A GLANCE**

FEATURES Zen temple with pond garden and dry landscape (*karesansui*).

ACCESS From Kyoto JR stn, city bus no. 73 to Kokederamichi (50 mins). Alternatively, from Matsuo stn on the Hankyu Arashiyama line, then 20 mins walk.

PRACTICALITIES Applications at least a week in advance with return postcard (*ofuku hagaki*) stating preferred date, name, address, number of people. (Search for 'Saiho-ji reservation' on the Internet.) Visit times are fixed and limited to 90 mins. Fee Y3000. Temple tel. (075)-391-3631.

FOUNDATION Temple tradition says eighth century by the priest Gyoki. Refounded 1339 by Muso Soseki.

RIGHT The pond is laid out in the shape of the Chinese ideogram for *kokoro* (heart-mind). It was originally part of a Pure Land garden but was converted by Muso Soseki into a Zen stroll garden.

BELOW The pleasing arrangement of natural materials that make up the water basin (*temizuya*), intended for hand and mouth purification prior to entering the garden, forms part of the overall aesthetics.

Saiho-ji is known popularly as Kokedera (Temple of Moss) on account of its famous garden, and to minimise the risk of damage to the sensitive plant the number of visitors is strictly controlled. Not only does the temple charge the highest entry fee in Kyoto, but on arrival visitors are requested to copy out a sutra (traceable from a master sheet). As this takes place in the Main Hall, it's a rare chance to experience a temple event although it's advisable not to spend too long on it.

The temple layout was designed by Muso Soseki (later abbot of Tenryu-ji), who converted run-down premises into a Zen temple. Over the centuries it suffered destruction on several occasions, and the buildings are consequently modern. Apart from the Main Hall built in 1969, there is a three-storey pagoda that dates from 1978. The garden, however, has survived in its original design.

The lower portion is arranged around a pond shaped as the Chinese character for *kokoro* (mind or heart). Here are displayed all the aesthetics of Japanese garden design, with rocks, pathways and bridges placed with delicate care as to their effect. Beneath the shade of the surrounding trees is a carpet of moss (specialists have

counted 120 different kinds), and the varying hues of green are at their best in the glistening damp of June and July.

On a slope above the pond is a teahouse and dry landscape garden (*karesansui*), near to which is a Meditation Rock on which it is said that Muso Soseki used to sit in contemplation. 'People who understand that streams, earth, plants, trees and rocks are all one with the fundamental self can use these natural features as part of their meditation,' he wrote. Looking down on the pond garden, one can't help but feel that it's a perfect reflection of his philosophy.

After an initial circumambulation to get the feel of the garden, it's good to go round again to take in the details. The 4.5 acres (1.8 hectares) contain several interesting features, including a Momoyama-era teahouse by the pond. It's said that originally the garden was covered in white sand and that the moss developed naturally due to a lack of maintenance. Now it's a striking exemplar of how gardens in Japan have been raised to an art form—one that is organic and ever-changing.

KOZAN-JI
A SECLUDED MEDITATIONAL RETREAT

**KOZAN-JI
AT A GLANCE**

FEATURES Shingon temple with Sekisui-in (former villa), Chojugiga scrolls, Japan's first tea field and wooded precincts.

ACCESS From Kyoto JR stn, JR bus to Kajinoo, about 50 mins.

PRACTICALITIES 9.00–17.00. Y600 (grounds free). Temple tel. (075) 861-4204. Allow about 1 hour. Visits can be combined with nearby Jingo-ji.

FOUNDATION 774, by temple tradition. Refounded 1206 by the monk Myoe

ABOVE RIGHT Sekisui-in, the sole original building to survive, has shutters that open upwards and outwards onto the natural surrounds in the manner of aristocratic villas of the past.

BELOW The founder of the temple, a nobleman named Myoe, meditated in trees and other outdoor places by way of rejecting the Zen style of meditating in a room.

Kozan-ji is located in the northwestern corner of Kyoto, on the lower slope of a wooded mountain. The area is noted for its summer breezes and autumn foliage. Most visitors head for nearby Jingo-ji, unaware of the quiet charm of Kozan-ji, a Buddhist temple of the Omuro sect. The temple owns a remarkable collection of Cultural Assets, including a document archive with Japan's oldest Chinese character dictionary.

The temple was founded by a well-born scholar-monk called Myoe (1173–1232). He is remembered for practising meditation in a tree, as depicted in a painting, and also for planting Japan's first tea field after being given seeds by his friend Eisai, who had brought them back from China. A restored tea field stands on the original site, and tea producers make an annual offering at the temple.

Architecturally, pride of place at Kozan-ji goes to the elegant Sekisui-in building. Once the study hall of retired Emperor Gotoba, it was relocated to serve as Myoe's private residence. With its gabled and shingled roof, it is a fine exemplar of the Kamakura style (1186–1333). When the shutters open onto the lush surrounds, the aristocratic refinement of the past is evident in the pleasing integration with nature.

Other temple buildings are modern reconstructions of the originals. The Kaisando, with bell-shaped windows, houses a famous bust of Myoe (not on display), and the Main Hall stands on its own amidst ancient cedars and maple trees. For those looking to combine a visit to a World Heritage Site with peace and a pleasant stroll, Kozan-ji may well be the perfect place.

ABOVE The porch of the Sekisui-in offers an example of the harmony with nature that characterised traditional Japanese architecture. The statue is of Prince Shotoku as a two-year-old child saying his first prayer.

RIGHT The Main Hall (Kondo) of Kozan-ji stands on its own in the woods, among tall cryptomeria trees. Inside is a statue of Yakushi Nyorai, dating from the early years of the temple.

The temple's most prized possession is a set of four scrolls known as Chojugiga, dating from the twelfth and thirteenth centuries. The first of the scrolls has a satire of priests and politicians in the guise of animals, which disport themselves in pompous manner, and the comical drawings have been hailed as a predecessor of modern *manga*. Though the originals are on loan to Tokyo National Museum, Kozan-ji displays a reproduction in Sekisui-in and sells images as postcards and on souvenirs.

WORLD HERITAGE SITES OF ANCIENT NARA

The Original Template for Japanese Civilisation

In the eighth century, when Heijo-kyo (Nara) was capital of Japan, the country underwent a transformation from a clan-based society to a centralised state with legal codes based on the Chinese system. The buildings of the period reflect the borrowings from the continent, and Korean craftsmen were often involved in the artwork.

After relocation of the court to Kyoto, the Heijo-kyo capital fell into decay. However, its great temples survived, as did Kasuga Shrine, thanks to patronage from on high. In later centuries, a new town developed around them, which became the basis of modern Nara.

The imperial palace of Heijo-kyo was for long covered over with rice fields, but excavations during the twentieth century revealed the remains underground. Now they form part of a World Heritage Site centered around Nara's time as capital. Remarkably, the great temples of the eighth century not only remain working institutions but have survived to be the leading examples in East Asia of the period's artistic and architectural achievements.

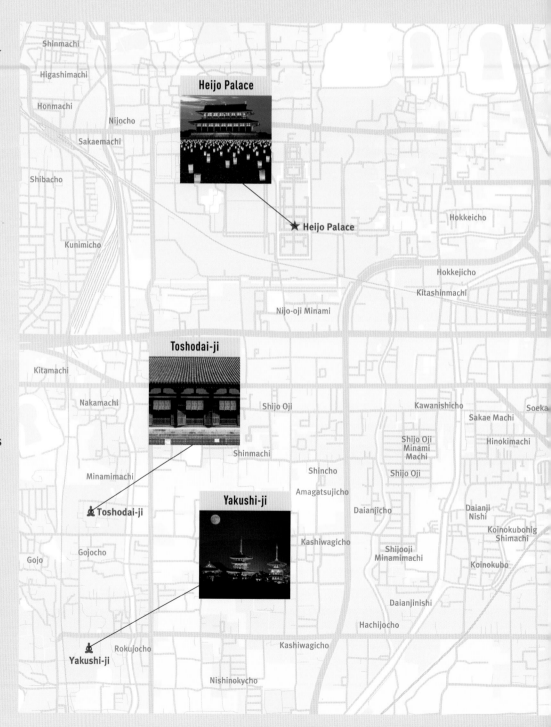

REGISTRATION 1998, as 'Historic Monuments of Ancient Nara'.

FEATURES 8 items (5 temples, a former palace, a shrine and sacred forest): Todai-ji, Toshodai-ji, Yakushi-ji, Gango-ji, Kofuku-ji, Heijo-kyo Palace, Kasuga Taisha and Kasuga Primeval Forest.

ACCESS 5 of the 8 properties are within walking distance of JR Nara or Kintetsu Nara stns. Toshodai-ji and Yakushi-ji lie close to Nishinokyo stn (Kintetsu line); Heijo-kyo is near Saidai-ji stn (also Kintetsu).

INFORMATION Nara City Tourist Information (at Kintetsu stn): (0742) 24-4858. Volunteer guides available (apply in advance). Allow a couple of days to see all.

DATELINE
710—Capital established at Heijo-kyo (Nara)
784—Capital moved to Nagaoka-kyo; 10 years later to Heian-kyo (modern Kyoto)

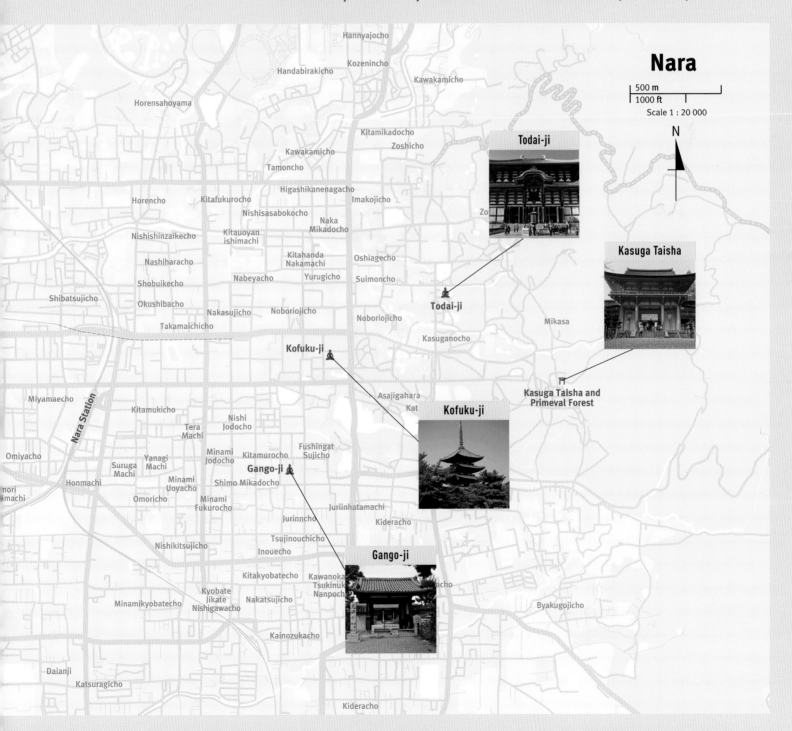

HEIJO PALACE

THE IMPERIAL COMPOUND OF ANCIENT NARA

FEATURES A compound over half a square
mile in size (1 km x 1.3 km), with foundations,
museums and reconstructions of Suzaku
Gate, Imperial Audience Hall and East Palace
Garden.

ACCESS From Kyoto, take the Kintetsu line
for Yamato-Saidaiji stn, then 20 mins walk.
From JR Nara stn, bus for 20 mins, or from
Kintetsu Nara for 15 mins. Summer shuttle
bus between JR Nara and Yamato-Saidaiji.

PRACTICALITIES 9.00–16.30 (closed Mon).
Free. Tel. Nara Palace Site (0742) 30-6753;
email: jimu@nabunken.go.jp. For detailed
information, see www.kkr.mlit.go.jp/asuka/
heijo/english/.

DURATION Allow half a day to see everything, including Heijo-kyo History Museum
(Y500; virtual reality movie), Nara Palace Site
Museum and Excavation Site Exhibition Hall
(free).

DATELINE
710—Foundation of Heijo-kyo
784—Capital moves to Nagaoka-kyo
794—Capital moves to Heian-kyo (Kyoto) and
   the Heijo Palace abandoned
1889—Location rediscovered
20th century—Excavations and reconstructions

The Heijo-kyo capital was modeled on
the grid system of the Chinese, oriented
towards the south in keeping with
feng-shui. The imperial compound, which
occupied about 5 percent of the city,
lay in the north and was off-limits to
ordinary citizens. It not only contained
the private residence of the emperor's
family but government offices and the
great ceremonial buildings of state. Here
was the heart of a newly formed country.

The compound originally had twelve
gates and was enclosed by earthen
ramparts. From the Suzaku Gate in the
south opened up a grand boulevard that
led to the Chodo-in (Hall of State) and
Daigokuden (Imperial Audience Hall).
Each building stood on a podium, with
tiled roof and vermilion pillars as in Tang

China. By contrast, the imperial residence
(Dairi) was in Japanese style with a
shingled roof and unpainted pillars set
into the ground.

In later centuries, when Kyoto was
capital, the abandoned site was used for
rice fields, but in 1889 the location was
rediscovered and its historical significance recognised. The twentieth century
saw major efforts at conservation (though
bizarrely a railway line runs across part
of the site), and excavations initiated in
the 1950s are still ongoing. The unearthed
remains were crucial to the World
Heritage recognition.

The site now has a park-like feel, with
museums and markers to indicate former
structures. There are also reconstructions,
which include the majestic Suzaku Gate

RIGHT The Suzaku Gate, now reconstructed, stood in the
south and marked the official entrance to the Heijo-kyo
capital. Foreign dignitaries were received here in welcome
ceremonies.

(1998), the East Palace Garden (1998), and the compound's most important building, the Imperial Audience Hall (2010), completed to coincide with the 1300th anniversary of Heijo-kyo's foundation. The dazzling interior, with a recreation of the emperor's throne, makes a magnificent centerpiece to a site that stands at the heart of Nara's time as capital.

ABOVE The reconstructed Imperial Audience Hall, which originally formed the heart of the Heijo-kyo capital, was the focus for the 1300th anniversary celebrations in 2010.

BELOW LEFT Inside the Imperial Audience Hall is a reconstruction of the imperial seat used for important meetings and ceremonies of state.

BELOW RIGHT The carefully recreated East Palace Garden was used by the imperial family for banquets and ceremonies. It is thought to be the prototype for later pond gardens.

TODAI-JI

HOUSING THE WORLD'S LARGEST BRONZE STATUE

**TODAI-JI
AT A GLANCE**

FEATURES Head temple of the Kegon sect with Daibutsuden (Hall of the Great Buddha), Nandaimon (Great South Gate), Shoro (Belfry), Nigatsudo (Second Month Hall), Hokke-do (Third Month Hall) and Shoso-in (Treasury).

ACCESS From Kintetsu Nara stn, 20 mins walk through Nara Park. From JR Nara stn, 30 mins walk or bus to Todaiji Daibutsuden.

PRACTICALITIES 7.30/8.00–16.30/17.30 (seasonal). Y500 (joint ticket with Museum Y800). Tel. (0742) 22-5511; fax (0742) 22-0808. Allow around 2 hours for all.

FOUNDATION 752, by Emperor Shomu.

ABOVE The seated gilt bronze Buddha is 49 feet (15 meters) tall and the right hand is raised in the gesture of preaching. The statue was financed by devotees who believed they would accrue spiritual benefit.

Todai-ji not only boasts the world's biggest bronze Buddha, but the world's largest wooden building from pre-modern times. The scale is astonishing: the ears of the Buddha alone are larger than a human being. The building that houses it is 157 feet (48 meters) tall and 187 feet (57 meters) long. (The original was even larger.) Fire and earthquake have damaged both Buddha and building over the centuries, but human resilience has ensured that they have always been restored. It is truly one of the world's great wonders.

The temple was founded by Emperor Shomu as the centerpiece in a network of provincial temples by which he planned to promote the well-being of the nation. The name, which means Great Eastern Temple, derived from its location to the east of the imperial palace. Tradition states that 2.6 million people were involved in the enterprise, which would have been half the entire population. More reliably, the project is known to have all but bankrupted the country because of the huge amounts of timber and bronze involved.

On completion, the statue was plated with gold and dedicated in a grand 'eye-opening ceremony' attended by some 10,000 people. A giant platform was erected on which an Indian priest painted in the eyes with an enormous brush, which is housed now in the temple's treasury along with the congratulatory gifts which came from as far afield as Europe along the Silk Road.

It took another forty-six years before the rest of the compound was finished,

RIGHT View from the Great Buddha Hall towards the Chumon Gate. The bronze octagonal lantern in the middle of the pathway has survived from the original temple.

BELOW The Daibutsuden or Great Buddha Hall dates from the middle of the Edo era (1603–1867). When it was first built in the eighth century, it was one-third bigger.

including two pagodas 328 feet (100 meters) tall, thought to have been the tallest structures in the world apart from the pyramids. (They were destroyed by earthquake and not rebuilt.) The building around the Buddha, known as the Daibutsuden, was also twice destroyed, the last occasion being in 1709. The reconstruction was 30 percent smaller but is nonetheless enormous: the roof alone has 110,000 tiles, each of which weighs 33 pounds (15 kg).

The approach to Todai-ji leads through a deer park popular with tourists, and the first feature to greet visitors is the magnificent Great South Gate (Nandaimon). It houses two Nio guardians, 26 feet

(8 meters) tall, carved in 1203. Beyond it, in front of the Great Buddha Hall, stands an enormous bronze octagonal lantern which was part of the original temple

Inside the hall is the seated bronze Buddha flanked by two attendants. It represents Birushana, chief deity of the Kegon sect of Buddhism. With a height of 49 feet (15 meters), it weighs over 500 tons yet manages to evoke a sense of serenity. The eyes are over 3 feet (1 meter) wide, the ears 8 feet (2.5 meters) long, and the hair made up of 966 bronze balls. The statue has been repaired on several occasions (in 855 it lost its head in an earthquake), but the lotus petal base and both legs have survived from the original.

At the back of the hall can be found a model of the original building, showing the pagodas. Another popular feature is a 'healing pillar' in the base of which is an opening the size of the Buddha's nostril. Crawling through it is said to bring salvation, and the challenge is often taken up by children and young adults to the delight of their friends.

Prominent amongst the temple's other buildings is the Shoso-in Warehouse, raised on pillars to protect its 9,000 precious items from damp. (It holds an annual exhibition at Nara National Museum.) A similar 'loghouse style' can be seen at the Kaidan-in Hall, rebuilt in 1733 and containing notable statues of the Four Deva Kings, while the Belfry (Shoro) contains the second biggest bell in Japan after Kyoto's Chion-in. A more recent addition is the Todai-ji Culture Center, opened in 2011, which displays some of the temple's treasures.

The Hokke-do (Lotus Hall) is of interest for combining two buildings from different eras (the eighth-century section is Todai-ji's oldest structure). Nearby is the Nigatsudo, which stands on a slope and offers a fine view of the city from its balcony. Every March it serves as the setting for the spectacular Omizutori Festival, when huge pine torches on the veranda scatter sparks over a packed crowd—surely a unique event for a World Heritage Site made of wood!

OPPOSITE TOP The Nigatsudo (February Hall) with its small guardian shrine is a subtemple on the Todai-ji precincts which offers fine views of Nara from its balcony.

OPPOSITE BOTTOM Priests waving enormous pine torches run along the balcony of the Nigatsudo during the Omizutori Festival in March. Sparks that fall over onlookers below are thought to signify a safe year for them.

LEFT The bronze Buddha, representing Birushana (Vairocana in Sanskrit), is flanked on either side by bodhisattva figures added in 1709. Represented here is the Kokuzo Bosatsu, deity of wisdom and memory.

BELOW The Kagami-ike (Mirror Pond) stands before the Dabutsuden compound, to the right of the Chumon Gate. Performances of Bugaku dance take place here during the Shomu Tenno-sai Festival in May.

KOFUKU-JI

THE TEMPLE OF HAPPINESS AND SYMBOL OF NARA

FEATURES Hosso sect temple with East Main Hall (Tokondo), Treasure House (Kokuhokan), 2 pagodas, Northern and Southern Octagonal Halls (Hokuendo, Nanen-do) and Oyuya bath house.

ACCESS Walk from Kintetsu Nara (5 mins) or JR Nara (20 mins) or bus from JR Nara to Kencho-mae (7 mins).

PRACTICALITIES 9.00–17.00. East Main Hall and Treasure House Y800, otherwise free. Tel. (0742) 22-7755. Allow about 1 hour.

DATELINE
669—Temple founded as Yamashina-dera
710—Relocation to Heijo-kyo as Kofuku-ji
1180—Destroyed in fighting. Partially rebuilt.
1881—Renovation initiated and reconstruction ongoing

FAR RIGHT The pagoda stands next to the East Main Hall and was rebuilt in 1426 following a fire. Arranged around its central pillar are a Yakushi triad, a Shaka triad, an Amida triad and a Miroku triad.

BELOW 'Cleanliness is next to godliness.' Though the expression comes from the Hebrew tradition, it applies just as much to Buddhism and the Japanese tradition.

Kofuku-ji was once one of Nara's great temples, which at its height had over 150 buildings. It was the family temple of the Fujiwara, who for centuries virtually ran the country. However, after the twelfth century when the samurai rose to power, the temple suffered a downturn and was ravaged by fire on five different occasions. By the time of the Meiji Restoration (1868) it was a shadow of its former self, but ongoing reconstruction is now recapturing the former grandeur; the Central Main Hall will be completed in 2018.

Pride of place goes to the temple's five-storey pagoda, which has become a symbol of Nara as a whole. First erected in 725, it was destroyed and rebuilt several times, the last occasion being 1426. At just over 164 feet (50 meters), the pagoda is the second tallest in Japan and like its counterparts was built entirely without nails.

The most imposing structure is the Tokondo (East Main Hall), which is a 1415 reconstruction. The original was erected by Emperor Shomu for recovery of his ailing aunt, as a consequence of which the hall houses the 'buddha of healing', Yakushi Nyorai. Protecting it are four directional guardians (Shitenno), each carved from a single trunk.

The oldest of the present buildings is the Northern Octagonal Hall (721, rebuilt 1210), which commemorates the temple's second founder, Fujiwara no Fuhito. Its counterpart is the Southern Octagonal Hall (813, rebuilt 1741), which is an important stage in West Japan's thirty-three temple pilgrimage. Both the Octagonal Halls hold statuary only rarely open for viewing.

In 1959, a museum was established which is 'a must see' for admirers of Buddhist art. Its prized possession is a wooden six-armed Ashura coated in dry lacquer. Another well-known item is a bronze head of Yakushi Nyorai. Kofuku-ji means Temple of Happiness, and after viewing such treasures it would be hard to leave without a smile.

RIGHT The temple originally had three main halls though only the East Main Hall remains. As well as the main image of Yakushi Nyorai, the hall contains several other valuable statues of Buddhist deities.

KASUGA TAISHA

AN ANCIENT SHINTO SHRINE SET IN A SACRED FOREST

FEATURES Shinto shrine with subshrines and primeval forest.

ACCESS From Kintetsu Nara or JR Nara stns, walk across the deer park (30–45 mins) or take the bus to Kasuga Taisha Honden (7–12 mins). Alternatively, 15 mins walk from Todai-ji.

PRACTICALITIES Inner Shrine 9.00–17.00 (seasonal variation). Y500. Free bilingual pamphlet available. Treasure House Y400; Botanical Gardens Y500. Outer area including Wakamiya Shrine and Meoto Daikokusha free. Tel. (0742) 22-7788; fax (0742) 27-2114. Allow 2 hours.

SPECIAL OCCASIONS Lantern light-ups at Setsubun (Feb 2–4) and Obon (Aug 14–15). Kasuga Matsuri (March 13) traditional arts. Wisteria in bloom (late April–early May). Onmatsuri at Wakamiya Jinja (Dec 15–17) featuring dance.

FOUNDATION Officially 768, though possibly c. 710.

Kasuga is one of Japan's foremost shrines. It is associated with the Fujiwara family, once the most powerful in the land, and is famous for its setting on the edge of Nara Park at the foot of two sacred hills. According to legend, the Fujiwara clan invited a powerful deity to Nara who arrived riding a deer, which is why the animal is regarded as sacred and allowed to wander at will around the grounds. Three other *kami* are enshrined at Kasuga, one of them the founding ancestor of the Fujiwara. For centuries the family held power by marrying their daughters to prospective emperors, so that even after the capital at Nara was abandoned Kasuga was able to survive thanks to imperial patronage.

In the late Heian Period (794–1185), the shrine came under the auspices of Kofuku-ji, the Fujiwara family temple. The Buddhists endorsed the sanctity of the deer by reference to the Deer Park in Benares, where the Buddha gave his first sermon after enlightenment. The animal was thus doubly blessed. At its height, the Shinto-Buddhist complex had 175 buildings and enormous influence, which only came to an end with the Meiji Restoration of 1868 when the new government separated the two religions.

RIGHT ABOVE A priest in traditional attire conducts a ritual in front of the altar. The four enshrined *kami* are connected with the central myths of Yamato and ancient Japan.

RIGHT BELOW The stone lanterns that line the pathway to the shrine were donated by worshippers of all classes to light the way for ancestral spirits. The Kasuga style of lantern is particularly ornate and bears the image of a deer.

OPPOSITE The free-roaming deer, one of which is here seen grazing in front of the shrine's Chumon Gate, are protected as familiars of the Kasuga *kami* and deepen the sense of communion with nature.

past by worshippers. Lighting a lantern was the customary way to greet the spirits of the dead. There are 2,000 stone lanterns in all, some of which are so immense that they dwarf the humans passing before them. There are a further 1,000 hanging bronze lanterns, so that the total matches the 3,000 Kasuga branch shrines throughout the country. When all of them are lit, which happens twice a year, the effect is spectacular.

Entrance to the shrine is through a Chumon Gate dating from 1613, to the left of which is a Japanese cedar estimated to be over 800 years old. The main compound, with its vermilion pillars, houses four sanctuaries, one for each of the *kami* enshrined. They exemplify the *kasuga-zukuri* style, which features a canopied entrance beneath a gabled roof. The design is thought to have originated in the eighth century and it was used as a model for many other shrines.

Up until then, the shrine maintained the *shikinen sengu* tradition of reconstructing its buildings every twenty years, in keeping with the notion of renewal that lies at the heart of Shinto.

The approach to Kasuga, which once began at Kofuku-ji, is lined with closely placed lanterns that were donated in the

Since Kasuga stands on the edge of a forest, the natural materials and cypress bark roof harmonise with the surrounds, exemplifying the Shinto thinking that

humans are an integral part of nature. The woods here have been sacred since 841 when hunting and tree felling were prohibited, and the only human intervention, apart from reforestation after typhoon damage, is in the form of footpaths; one leads up the hill past stone statues and waterfalls.

Around the main shrine are other items of interest. Wakamiya Jinja, built in the same style, is an auxiliary shrine founded in 1135, opposite which is the Meoto Daikokusha housing a pair of married deities associated with matchmaking. Kasuga also owns a Treasure Hall containing precious artifacts, many of which were Heian-era imperial offerings such as mirrors, masks, decorated weaponry and musical instruments.

The Botanical Garden features 250 plants from the Nara Period, as well as a section containing 20 different types of wisteria, a shrine symbol since Fujiwara

translates as 'field of wisteria'. Next door is the Nintai Tearoom, built in the eighteenth century, which serves Manyo porridge eaten in Nara times. In this way, the shrine and its surrounds offer the perfect opportunity to breathe and 'digest' the atmosphere of the eighth century when Heijo-kyo was the country's capital and Nara formed an end point for the Silk Road.

ABOVE The main entrance to the shrine is through the Nanmon (South Gate), which gives onto an outer compound open to visitors. The inner compound containing the sanctuaries for the *kami* requires a fee.

LEFT The cinnamon red coloring of the corridors, together with the white plastered walls, provides a bright happy atmosphere and is typical of the Kasuga style.

BELOW Raking and sweeping the grounds are part of the Shinto ethic of purity, which goes along with diligence, sincerity and service to the *kami*.

YAKUSHI-JI

A SEVENTH-CENTURY TEMPLE RESTORED TO ITS FORMER GRANDEUR

OPPOSITE ABOVE The Main Hall (Kondo), rebuilt in the 1970s, is flanked by two pagodas as it would have been in the original temple. The arrangement is known as the Yakushi style.

OPPOSITE BELOW The East and West Pagodas have similar but not identical structures. Although they seem to have six storeys, they are, in fact, three-storeyed with extra roofs inserted.

Before Nara, the capital city was at Fujiwara-kyo, about 13 miles (20 km) away. In 680, Emperor Tenmu planned a temple there for his ailing wife, which was dedicated to the 'Buddha of healing', Yakushi Nyorai. As it turned out, the emperor died before his wife, who completed construction of the temple as Empress Jito. Following removal of the capital to Nara in 710, the temple was relocated and enlarged, becoming one of the 'Seven Great Temples of Nara'.

Fire destroyed the temple on several occasions, the most devastating being in 1528. Some structures were rebuilt, but the temple went into decline and by the twentieth century little remained of the original except the striking East Pagoda. A restoration campaign was launched in the 1970s, and with the help of millions of individual donations the main buildings have been rebuilt on their original sites. As a result, the symmetrical layout of the temple can now be fully appreciated; Yakushi-ji was, in fact, the first to employ an East and West Pagoda.

The Kondo or Main Hall was rebuilt in the 1970s after damage by fire. Such halls typically had a clay floor and open attic space, but here a wooden floor and ceiling provide a warmer feeling. The hall houses a Yakushi triad of bronze statues considered among the best of their age, brought to Nara from the original temple. Once they were gilded, but in the fire of 1528 they were blackened by flames. Instead of holding a small medicine jar, as is usual, the Yakushi figure here sits on a medicine chest, which in its decorative motifs shows clear Silk Road influences.

Behind the statue is a stone relief of the Buddha's footprints, which in the middle ages were a popular focus of veneration. Larger than life, they are 18.5 inches (47 cm) long and bear auspicious symbols. Next to them is a tablet with twenty-one verses of praise that were sung by medieval worshippers and which feature in Japanese literature.

The magnificent Toindo (East Hall) is a late thirteenth-century reconstruction, standing on a base to protect it from water damage. It contains a bronze image of Shokannon, 6.3 feet (1.90 meters) high, which was a seventh-century gift from the king of Paekche in Korea. Placed around it are four Shitenno guardians, colored according to the direction they protect.

The temple's highlight is the East Pagoda, which is the only surviving eighth-century structure. Just over 108 feet (33 meters) high, it appears to have six storeys whereas, in fact, there are only three and the others are inter-storey pent roofs (*mokoshi*). At the top is a distinctive globe-shaped bronze filial 33 feet (10 meters) high, which not only lends stability but acts as a lightning rod. The pagoda's design has been widely admired, and the American art expert, Ernest Fenollosa, famously described it as 'frozen music'. Considered one of the country's very finest, the pagoda continues to delight visitors nearly 1,300 years after construction.

In the temple's Treasury are Buddhist statues, paintings, screens, calligraphy and documents, many from the eighth century. The most prized item is a painting on hemp cloth depicting a celestial maiden called Kichijoten in a delicate flowing dress. Said to be modeled on Empress Komyo, it is considered a religious icon and only exhibited for brief periods.

Yakushi-ji is the head temple of the Hosso sect, based on the teachings of a seventh-century Chinese monk known as Ganjo Sanzo. In 1942, the remains of the monk were found by Japanese soldiers in Nanjing, and later part of them were enshrined in the Ganjo-Sanzoin compound (open in spring and autumn). The centerpiece is an octagonal Mausoleum, beyond which is a building with paintings by celebrated artist Hirayama Ikuo depicting the monk's travels to India and Central Asia. Considering the Silk Road connections of Yakushi-ji, it is a fitting addition to the temple's rich and multicultural heritage.

107

LEFT ABOVE While the West Pagoda looks resplendent, the more ancient East Pagoda is currently undergoing extensive reconstruction that will last until 2019.

LEFT BELOW Constructed in 1981, the Octagonal Hall is in a complex dedicated to the seventh-century Chinese monk Ganjo Sanzo, some of whose remains are enshrined here.

TOP Roof detail showing an *onigawara* (demon tile), the fearsome looks of which are designed to scare away evil spirits and remind onlookers to behave themselves.

ABOVE MIDDLE Detail from the replica medicine chest beneath the Yakushi Nyorai image in the Main Hall, showing notable influences from India and the Silk Road.

ABOVE Unlike the gilded statuary elsewhere, the Buddha figure here has been blackened by smoke after surviving the great fire that destroyed the building around it.

TOSHODAI-JI
THE LARGEST SURVIVING STRUCTURE FROM THE NARA PERIOD

FEATURES A Risshu sect temple with Kondo (Main Hall), Kodo (Lecture Hall), Shariden (Relic Hall), Koro (Bell Tower), Hozo and Kyozo (Repositories), Miedo (Memorial Hall).

ACCESS From Kintetsu Nara stn, train to Nishinokyo stn (10 mins) and walk for 2 mins. Alternatively, bus 70, 72 or 97 from JR Nara (15 mins) or Kintetsu Nara (20 mins). The temple lies 500 meters from Yakushi-ji.

PRACTICALITIES 8.30–16.30 (last entry). Y600 (plus Y100 for Treasury). Temple tel. (0742) 33-7900. Allow up to 2 hours.

FOUNDATION 759, by the Chinese monk Ganjin.

Toshodai-ji is closely tied to the development of Buddhism in Japan, for a whole generation of priests owed their training to its Chinese founder, Ganjin. He was invited to Japan by Emperor Shomu, but it took twelve years and five aborted attempts before he managed the crossing from China. By that time he was sixty-six years old and had lost his eyesight. Nonetheless, after an initial period at Todai-ji he was able to solicit sufficient funds for the establishment of Toshodai-ji; appropriately, the name means 'Invited from Tang China'. He lies buried in an attractive moss-covered grove at the back of the temple.

The Main Hall is the largest building to survive intact from the Nara Period (710–84). With eight front pillars, swollen at their middle, it has been compared to the Parthenon of Greece, and thanks to recent renovation it can be appreciated in all its magnificence. Behind it stands a Lecture Hall, which started life as the Nara capital's State Assembly Hall, the only part of the old imperial compound to survive. Like the Main Hall, the Lecture Hall has undergone extensive restoration, which lasted ten years and involved complete dismantlement.

The only two-storey building on the site, known as Shariden, contains relics of the Buddha brought from China by Ganjin. Also of interest are two 'log-house style' repositories called Hozo and Kyozo that were built for storing scrolls.

In addition, there are sleeping quarters for the monks, a stone ordination platform, a large belfry and a temple museum. With its 17 National Treasures and 200 Important Cultural Properties, Toshodai-ji is more than just a temple. It is a monument to the great flourishing of religious art that took place during Nara's time as capital of Japan.

OPPOSITE Toshodai-ji's Main Hall (Kondo) is not only the largest but one of the most graceful buildings to survive from the Nara Period. Behind it stands another impressive long building, the Kodo (Lecture Hall).

ABOVE Toshodai-ji once had 48 subtemples but now offers a relatively calm atmosphere compared to its more popular neighbor, Yakushi-ji. To the left can be seen the temple's belfry, while to the right is the two-storey Koro or reliquary and former monks' sleeping quarters.

RIGHT The impressive woodwork of the Main Hall has won many admirers, and the building was much praised in poems of the past. With its row of pillars, the hall has also been compared to the Parthenon.

BELOW The burial mound for Ganjin is at the back of the temple precinct in grounds of its own. He died aged 76, and a statue of him made by his disciples stands in the Miedo.

GANGO-JI

JAPAN'S EARLIEST BUDDHIST TEMPLE

FEATURES A Shingon-Ritsu temple with
Gokurakubo (Main Hall), Zenshitsu (Zen
room), Museum and garden with 2,500
memorial stones.

ACCESS From Kintetstu Nara or JR Nara
stns, about 15 mins walk.

PRACTICALITIES 9.00–17.00 (closed
Dec 29–Jan 4). Y400. Tel. (0742) 23–1376.
Allow up to 1 hour.

DATELINE
593—Hoko-ji built in Asuka (also Asuka-dera)
718—Relocation to Heijo-kyo and renamed
1451—Temple mostly burnt down

In 588, the powerful clan leader Soga no
Umako ordered construction in Asuka,
then the capital city, of a Buddhist temple
called Hoko-ji. It was an historic event,
for it marked acceptance of the foreign
faith by the country's élite. Upon completion in 593, it was known popularly as the
Asuka Temple (Asuka-dera). It was to be
the first of thousands.

Following the establishment of a new
capital at Heijo-kyo (Nara), the decision
was taken to relocate the Asuka Temple.
It was set up to the east of the imperial
compound and enlarged, with seven halls
and pagodas. Renamed Gango-ji, it
became one of the Seven Great Temples
of Nara. However, decline set in after
Kyoto became the capital in 794, and

devastating fires in the fifteenth and
nineteenth centuries all but destroyed
the complex.

The present temple, greatly reduced
in size, is of historical significance and
boasts three National Treasures. The first
is the Main Hall, constructed out of the
old priests' quarters in the Kamakura
Period (1186–1333). Some of the roof
tiles—those of a distinctive color—date
back to the original building in Asuka.
The Zen Room also offers a link to Japan's
first ever temple, for it was similarly
reconstructed from the old priests'
quarters and testing has confirmed the
wood was cut in the late sixth century.

The third of the National Treasures is
a miniature pagoda 18 Feet (5.5 meters)

RIGHT The modest entrance gate to Gango-ji was
originally part of a much grander complex containing
pagodas and seven halls. It covered the area now known
as Nara-machi, but fires in the fifteenth and nineteenth
centuries mostly destroyed it.

TOP Unusually, the Main Hall or Gokurakudo does not contain a statue as its main object of worship, but instead Chiko's Mandala. Chiko was a Nara-era abbot and his mandala won great popularity in medieval times.

ABOVE In former times, the temple was known for its Pure Land teachings and the temple museum houses an Amida statue. There is also a statue of Yakushi Nyorai, otherwise known as the Buddha of healing.

ABOVE LEFT The colored tiles covering part of the Main Hall and neighboring Zenshitsu were brought here from the original sixth-century temple. It is believed they were the first Korean-style tiles to be made in Japan.

high, prized as an authentic Nara-era structure. It is housed in the Treasury, which lies beyond an unusual Jizo garden featuring some 2,500 memorial stones laid out in rows, where a lantern festival is held at Obon. The area around Gango-ji, which once formed part of the temple, is the town's old merchants' quarter and makes for a pleasant stroll away from the crowds. Although the temple may not impress like Nara's other sites, it has a quiet charm and historical importance that transports one back in time to before Heijo-kyo even existed.

HORYU-JI

JAPAN'S OLDEST WOODEN BUILDINGS

REGISTRATION 1993, as 'Buddhist Monuments in the Horyu-ji Area'. It thereby became Japan's first World Heritage Site.

FEATURES A Shotoku sect monastic complex of 48 listed buildings in two parts: Sai-in (West Temple) houses a 5-storey pagoda and Kondo (Main Hall). To-in (East Temple) houses the Yumedono (Hall of Dreams). Also listed is Hokki-ji, under Horyu-ji auspices, a short taxi ride away.

ACCESS From JR Nara stn, 12 mins by train to Horyu-ji stn, then 20 mins walk.

PRACTICALITIES 8.00–17.00 (16.30 Nov–Feb). Y600. Taxi, map and rental bikes at the JR station. Temple tel. (0745) 75-2555. For tourist info, email ikaruga@kcn.ne.jp (free tours by volunteer guides in English). Allow at least 2 hours.

DATELINE
607—Founded by Prince Shotoku
670—Temple burnt down
c. 710—Rebuilding completed
739—Construction of To-in early 12th
　century
1374, 1603, mid-20th century—major
　repairs and restoration

OPPOSITE ABOVE The Main Hall of Horyu-ji is the graceful Kondo, which houses a Shaka triad as the temple's principal object of worship. The railings that skirt the upper level are decorated with Buddhist swastika patterns, typical of the Asuka style, as are the inverted V-shaped support posts.

OPPOSITE BELOW The Chumon or Central Gate formed the entrance to the Sai-in (Western Precinct). It is different in style from later gates, with four bays and an upper storey notably smaller in length than the lower.

Of the tens of thousands of Buddhist temples in Japan, Horyu-ji is the most significant because of its great antiquity, beauty and architectural integrity. Nearly the whole complex has been preserved, not just a single building. It was founded during the formative period in Japanese history when the country borrowed heavily from the advanced cultures of China and Korea. In later times there developed a more indigenous style, but here is a classic exemplar of Japan's ability to adopt and adapt. More than just a temple, Horyu-ji is a record of building styles from the seventh century onwards.

Buddhism arrived in Japan in 538 (some say 552), when an envoy from the Korean kingdom of Paekche introduced the faith. With it came an array of technical skills, which led to a new age of cultural development. By 624 there were 46 temples, and the showpiece was Horyu-ji, with its stunning statuary. The continental models on which the Japanese temple was based have not survived, so it remains the prime representative of early East Asian architecture.

The main compound houses two celebrated structures: the Pagoda and the Main Hall (Kondo). They stand side by side, unlike the Chinese style in which the buildings were aligned with the entrance. The beautifully proportioned pagoda served as the temple's reliquary, and its massive central pillar stands over 100 feet tall (30.5 meters). The two-storey Main Hall displays superb exterior woodwork, conspicuous amongst which are decorative dragons, a water deity thought to help prevent fire. Inside is

an evocation of the Buddhist paradise, with bronze Buddhas protected by Four Heavenly Guardians and surrounded by murals, replicas of the originals which were destroyed by fire in 1949.

In the temple's Treasury are some prized exhibits, such as a strikingly slender Kudara Kannon statue. Another famous item is the small Tamamushi Shrine, with its rows of minuscule ivory Buddhas. There are also posthumous portraits of the temple's founder, Prince Shotoku (572–622), which show him in idealised form. Appointed regent to his aunt, Empress Suiko, he was responsible for the country's first constitution in 604, and to many he remains a saintly figure who almost single-handedly spread Buddhism in Japan.

Horyu-ji's other compound, known as To-in, was built in 739 on the site of Shotoku's palace. At its center stands the Yumedono (Hall of Dreams), a delightful octagonal building which rises from a double stone terrace. The main image is the Guze Kannon, for long the most

hidden of all Japan's 'hidden Buddhas', the idea being that the spiritual power of an image is enhanced by restricting its exposure to the public. The statue was kept wrapped in silk until 1884, when it was uncovered at the insistence of Ernest Fenellosa, an American art expert with a remit from the Meiji government. What he found was a beautifully preserved statue, gilded and thought to resemble Shotoku himself.

A short taxi ride away from Horyu-ji lies the temple of Hokki-ji, which was founded in 622 by Shotoku's son. It is laid out in similar manner to Horyu-ji, though curiously the positioning of the pagoda and main hall is reversed. The temple was destroyed in the political disturbances of the sixteenth century and the only original structure to survive is a three-storey pagoda, built in 708. Together with its mother temple, it bears testimony to the cultural impact of Buddhism at a time when Japan was emerging as a unified state. It can truly be said that here history is written in wood.

ABOVE In addition to its pleasing proportions, Horyu-ji's Pagoda is considered a marvel of architectural design with in-built earthquake protection. It stands on a double terrace and has similar design features to the Main Hall.

BELOW The Daikodo or Lecture Hall was rebuilt in 990 following a fire and differs in style from earlier buildings. It houses a statue of Yakushi Nyorai flanked by two bodhisattvas, Nikko and Gekko.

Architectural features of the Asuka Age (538–710)

- slight curvature of columns (entasis), suggestive of Silk Road connections
- railings shaped in the manner of the Buddhist swastika symbol
- load-bearing wooden block plates at the top of corridor columns
- wooden bracket arms with cloud patterns to support the heavy tiled roofs

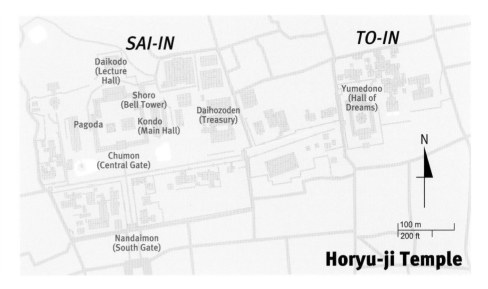

SAI-IN

Daikodo (Lecture Hall)

Shoro (Bell Tower)

Pagoda

Kondo (Main Hall)

Daihozoden (Treasury)

Chumon (Central Gate)

TO-IN

Yumedono (Hall of Dreams)

N

100 m
200 ft

Nandaimon (South Gate)

Horyu-ji Temple

ABOVE The Sai-in and To-in (West and East Temples) lie a few minutes walk apart. In between is the Daihozoden (Treasury), containing such famous treasures as the Kudara Kannon, the Dream-changing Kannon, the Tamamushi Shrine and portraits of Prince Shotoku.

LEFT The Yumedono is the oldest octagonal building in Japan, and its double terrace is characteristic of the Asuka Period. Inside is the Guze Kannon, believed to be a likeness of Prince Shotoku and only displayed for a month each spring and autumn.

BELOW The Shoro (Bell Tower) stands in the Eastern Precinct near the Yumedono (Hall of Dreams) and is notable for its 'spreading skirt' lower portion. It houses a bell dating from the Nara Period (710–84).

WORLD HERITAGE SITES OF THE KII PENINSULA

Sacred Sites Lying Along Ancient Pilgrimage Trails

REGISTRATION 2004, as a cultural landscape representing 'an extraordinary tradition of sacred mountains'.

FEATURES 3 areas (Mt Koya, Yoshino-Omine and Kumano) and connecting pilgrim routes (4 branches of Kumano Kodo, Choishimichi at Koya and Omineokugake-michi from Yoshino to Kumano).

INFORMATION Kumano Tourism: 0739-26-9025. Website with maps, routes and timetables: www.tb-kumano.jp/en. For Koyasan and Kumano volunteer guides: fumio909441@leto.eonet.ne.jp

PRACTICALITIES Access between areas is not easy (Koya to Kumano takes over 4 hours). Allow at least 3 days, more if trekking.

With its forested mountains, deep gorges and streams, the Kii Peninsula has been a spiritual heartland since ancient times. It was here that, according to myth, the founder of the imperial line, Emperor Jimmu, embarked on a campaign of conquest by landing on the coast and marching across the mountains to the Yamato River basin. In medieval times, it became Japan's foremost pilgrimage destination, and today it still continues to draw worshippers as well as large numbers of visitors to its ancient sites.

The World Heritage Site covers three separate areas. In simplistic terms, it could be said that Kumano represents Shinto, Mt Koya Buddhism and Yoshino-Omine Shugendo mountain asceticism. Although the areas evolved independently, they are spiritually linked and physically connected by pilgrimage routes. Taken together, they represent Japan's religious world view.

This is one of only two World Heritage Sites to feature pilgrimage routes, the other being Santiago de Compostela in Spain. The trails are steeped in history, with monuments and natural phenomena that have served since ancient times as objects of worship. Some routes lead over perilous terrain well over 3,300 feet (1,000 meters) high, but others consist of pleasant pathways through dense woodland. For the weary walker, there are hot springs to soothe the aching muscles, one of several attractive aspects to the area which have won it increasing attention in recent years.

Kyotanba   Aisho   Aisai

Sasayama   Nantan   Omihachiman   Higashiomi   Yatomi

           Nantan   Toin   Kisosaki
                      Kameoka   Ryuo   Hino   Komono
     Nose   Nagaokakyo   **Kyoto** Otsu Ritto   Kawagoe
Inagwa   Toyono   ⊙   Kusatsu   Kameyama   **YOKKAICHI**
Sanda   Yawata Uji   Suzuka
     Kawanishi   Takatsuki   Joyo   Wazuka   **Tsu**
Takarazuka   Minoo   Kyotanabe   Ide Seika Kasagi Minamiyamashiro Iga   ⊙
           Nishinomiya Katano   Kizugawa   Matsusaka
Kobe Ashiya **Osaka** Kadoma   Yamazoe   Meiwa
                Higashiosaka Daito   **Nara**   Taki   Tamaki
                      Yao   ⊙   Ise
           Fujidera   Ando Tenri   Nabari
                      Oji Kawai   Uda   Soni
     Tadaoka   Yamatotakada Kashihara   Mitsue
Kawachinagano   Gose   Sakurai   Odai
     Chihayaakasaka   Higashiyoshino   Daiki
Tajiri Kumatori   Yoshino ⊙   Kawakami
Hannan   Hashimoto Oyodo ★ Omine
Misaki   Katsuragi   Tenkawa
Wakayama ⊙ Iwade Kinokawa Koya ⊙
           Kimino   ★   Kamikitayama   Kihoku
Kainan   Nosegawa   Owase
Arida   Aridagawa
Hirogawa   Totsukawa   Shimokitayama
Hidaka Hidakagawa   Kitayama
Mihama   ⊙ Kumano
Gobo   Hongu ★   Mihama
     Inami   Kiho
     Minabe   Nachi ★ Shingu
Tanabe ⊙ Kamitonda   ★
Shirahama   Nachikatsuura
           Susami
                Kozagawa
           Kushimoto   Kii Oshima Island

MOUNT KOYA

SACRED HEADQUARTERS FOR THE SHINGON SECT OF BUDDHISM

**MOUNT KOYA
AT A GLANCE**

FEATURES A Shingon Buddhist complex. At the mountain base: Jison-in Temple, Niukanshofu Shrine and Niutsuhime Shrine. On the mountain: Kongobu-ji head temple, including Daimon Gate, Danjo Garan precinct, Tokugawa Mausolea, Kongo Sammai-in Monastery and Okunoin Cemetery. The Choishimichi pilgrimage route connects base and top.

ACCESS From Osaka Namba stn, Nankai line to Gokurakubashi (75 mins), transfer to cable car (5 mins), then bus to Kongobu-ji (10 mins). Rental car recommended for other properties.

INFORMATION Tourist Association (0736) 56-2616. Maps, rental bikes, audio guides (Y500) at the office near Kongobu-ji. Also Koyasan Crosscultural Communication Network (0736) 56-2270.

PRACTICALITIES Kongubu-ji 8.30–17.00. Y500. Koyasan World Heritage Ticket: Y3310 (15% off Nankai train and selected temples). Koyasan can be visited in a day, but temple lodging recommended (see http://eng.shukubo.net/).

FOUNDATION 816, by Kukai (known posthumously as Kobo Daishi).

Mt Koya or Koyasan is a complex of temples on a plateau 2,690 feet (820 meters) above sea level. It comprises the headquarters of the Shingon sect of Buddhism, and the location was intended to facilitate training in austerity, removed from the secular world. In the past, the complex was much bigger, making it one of the world's great mountain temples. Religious practice has been carried out here for 1,200 years, and for visitors it is a rare chance to experience the essence of Japanese spirituality.

The temple was founded by the legendary Kukai (774–835), who was not only an illustrious monk and proselytiser but a father figure of Japanese culture. Amongst his many virtues was excellence in calligraphy and sculpture, in addition

to which he carried out good works and taught practical skills to the peasantry. As founder of the Shingon sect, he is a revered figure at Koyasan and his statues are the focus of devotion.

The World Heritage Site comprises Kukai's original project, for which Jison-in at the base of the mountain acted as administrative base. Until 1872 Koyasan was a male-only mountain, and for centuries female pilgrims made the temple their end point (tradition has it that Kukai's own mother died in residence). As a result, female concerns are prominent, such as easy childbirth and protection from breast cancer.

A striking pagoda stands outside the compound, next to which a flight of stairs leads to Niukanshofu Shrine dedicated to

RIGHT The pagoda of Jison-in stands at the bottom of a flight of stairs marking the beginning of the Choishimichi trail that leads from the temple up the mountain to the plateau on which Kukai founded his monastery.

RIGHT Within the Okunoin Cemetery lies Gobyobashi, the bridge that leads to Kukai's mausoleum. The area is considered sacred, and after crossing the bridge visitors are asked not to drink, smoke, eat or take photographs.

BELOW The Kondo (Main Hall) of Kongobu-ji is where major services are held. The present structure, dating from 1932, is notable for the fire measures in place, namely a ladder and two large buckets of water on the curved roof.

Koyasan's guardian spirit. Legend tells how Kukai was looking for a suitable site when he came across a hunter, whose two dogs, one black and one white, led him to a hidden valley. The hunter turned out to be son of the Koya goddess, who granted him permission to use the land.

From Jison-in, a pilgrimage route called the Choishimichi runs up to the mountain complex. It takes about eight hours, and there are 180 stone markers where pilgrims stop to pray. The route passes near to Niutsuhime Jinja, which also enshrines the Koyasan goddess. The approach features a beautifully arched bridge over a koi pond, and within the compound are four fine sanctuaries.

The giant Daimon Gate that stands at the end of the pilgrim trail marks the access to the Danjo Garan precinct, where the monastery originated. The compound comprises some twenty imposing structures, including three pagodas, laid out like an open-air museum set around a pond garden. The site of Kukai's residence is marked by a memorial hall, and the main focus of worship is in the central pagoda with its Buddhist statuary.

A short walk away stands Kongobu-ji, constructed in 1593 and now Koyasan's head temple. It boasts a massive shingle roof, for the protection of which buckets of water and a ladder stand ready. (Nearly every building at Koya has been destroyed at some stage by fire.) Inside are spacious tatami rooms, one with paintings by master artist Kano Tanyu, and a modern wing has a retelling of the life story of Kobo Daishi as well as the largest rock garden in Japan.

LEFT TOP The Niutsuhime Shrine, which lies off the Choishimichi pilgrim trail, is surprisingly well-endowed with a carp pond, arched bridge and large two-storeyed Offertory.

LEFT MIDDLE Within the large Daimon entrance gate at the top of the Choishimichi pilgrim trail are Nio guardian figures, whose fearsome poses are designed to ward off evil spirits.

LEFT BOTTOM A Shinto priest reads out a *norito* prayer at the Niukanshofu Shrine, which stands at the bottom of the mountain and is dedicated to its goddess.

Under the temple's auspices are two ornate Tokugawa mausolea and a small monastery called Kongo Sammai-in. But for many, the most memorable aspect of Koyasan is the atmospheric Okunoin Cemetery, where amongst massive 1,000-year-old cedar trees are grave stones interspersed with stupas and quaintly bibbed Jizo. The site contains over 200,000 monuments, including tombs of famous figures. Towards the rear stands the mausoleum of Kukai himself, hallowed ground for believers, and a memorial hall called Torodo, with over 10,000 illuminated lanterns.

The Koya experience would not be complete without an overnight stay. It not only enables visitors to enjoy the vegetarian *shojin-ryori* eaten by monks but to attend the early morning chanting of sutras. If you follow it with a walk in Okunoin, you might feel that Kukai's mountain retreat was indeed blessed by the Koya goddess. It is a rare opportunity to gain an insight into Japanese religiosity while enjoying the very special atmosphere of a World Heritage Site.

TOP The main structure in the Danjo Garan precinct is the Daito Pagoda, which seems to have two storeys but only contains one. The original was founded in 816 but the present structure dates from 1937 following a fire. Inside is an arrangement of statues and paintings representing the mandalas of Shingon Buddhism.

ABOVE LEFT, MIDDLE AND BOTTOM The Okunoin Cemetery contains many Jizo statues because of the figure's role in guiding the spirits of the dead. The bodhisattva is traditionally depicted in the form of a monk with shaved head, holding a staff. It is the custom in Japan to clothe the statues, even sometimes to give them make-up, as a form of veneration. Red bibs are particularly common since Jizo is the guardian of children and red was thought to protect against illness. Some statues, such as those in the upper right picture, are for splashing with water, which is thought to fulfil wishes for the souls of the dead.

KUMANO

A POPULAR PILGRIMAGE ROUTE THROUGH
A FABLED SPIRITUAL LANDSCAPE

**KUMANO
AT A GLANCE**

FEATURES 3 shrines, 2 temples and
pilgrimage routes: Kumano Hayatama
Shrine, Kumano Hongu Shrine, Kumano
Nachi Shrine; Seiganto-ji and Fudarakusan-ji Temples; Kumano Sankeimichi (3
branches), Iseji and Omine Okugakemichi
pilgrimage routes.

ACCESS From Osaka 4 hours by JR train
to Shingu. Hongu is about 1 hour by bus
to the north. Rental car recommended for
other properties.

DURATION The properties can be visited
by car in 1 full day. Hiking the pilgrimage
routes can require days (see below).

INFORMATION Kumano Tourist Info
(0739) 33-7451. For public transport and
4-day trekking plan, see www.tb-kumano.
jp/en.

PRACTICALITIES Shrines are free (Nachi
Y300 for viewing platform, Seiganto-ji Y200
for pagoda). Tsuboyu hot spring 6.00–
21.30. Y750 (wait-your-turn system).

**Kumano is an area in the south of the
Kii Peninsula** known for its three great
shrines called the Kumano Sanzan.
Though their origin is obscure, they are
associated with Japan's early animism.
Hayatama Shrine originated with a
huge sacred rock, Nachi Shrine deifies
a waterfall and Hongu Shrine used to
stand on an islet in the Kumano River.
Mountains and water were crucial in
shaping Japan's spirituality, as were the
woods surrounding the shrines. Both
Hayatama and Nachi have sacred trees
over 800 years old.

The three shrines have a distinctive
style of architecture, with *chigi* cross-
beams and horizontal *katsuogi* logs on
the roof. The bright vermilion woodwork
together with the shingled roofs (rather
than tile) lend the buildings a prosperous
and attractive yet natural air. Although
tourists have largely displaced pilgrims,
the shrines remain lively spiritual centers
for study and meditation.

Common to all three shrines is the
motif of a three-legged crow (*yatagarasu*),
which in Shinto mythology is sent by the
sun goddess to guide Emperor Jimmu
across the region. There are various
theories as to its meaning, but the
accepted view is that it refers to an
ancestral ally of the imperial line. (The
three-legged crow has been adopted as
the symbol of Japan's football team.)

In the middle ages, the area's nature
worship was overlaid with Buddhism,
which saw in the mountains a spiritual
geography in the form of mandala. The
religions became fused into a Shinto-
Buddhist synthesis according to which
kami were regarded as local avatars of
universal Buddhist deities. This led to the
formation of temple-shrine complexes,
which lasted until the Meiji Restoration
of 1868 when the government separated
the two religions.

The legacy is best seen at Nachi, where
the route through the shrine leads
straight into the temple compound of
Seiganto-ji. The neighboring institutions
share a focus on Japan's largest waterfall,
436 feet (133 meters) high. While the
shrine has a separate platform for direct
worship of the waterfall, Seiganto-ji has a

RIGHT Pilgrims make their way down the steps to the
viewing platform for Nachi Waterfall. In days past, it would
have marked the culmination of an arduous trek but
nowadays most travel by bus and the amount of walking
is limited.

OPPOSITE The Seiganto-ji Pagoda is perfectly positioned
for views of Nachi Waterfall. Before the Meiji Restoration
of 1868, the temple was part of the Nachi Shrine and it
forms an important part of West Japan's 33 Kannon
Pilgrimage.

ABOVE A model of the boat in which the abbots of Fudarakusan-ji set out into the Pacific on their suicide missions to reach Kannon, the deity of compassion, thought to dwell in the south.

RIGHT A woman poses in costume on one of the many pathways that comprise the Kumano Kodo. The Old Roads consist of a network of trails, some of which run along the coast and some of which traverse high mountains.

FAR RIGHT Kumano Nachi Grand Shrine is located on the holy hill of Mt Nachi, though originally it stood at the foot of the nearby waterfall. It is known for its fire festival, when twelve huge pine torches and *mikoshi* (portable shrines) are carried down steep steps to the falls.

BELOW Kumano Hongu Grand Shrine used to stand on a sandbank of the Kumano River, but after being flooded in 1889 it was reconstructed in its present position on a small hill.

pagoda boasting a magnificent view. The wooded surrounds make the immersion in nature a prime example of Japan's spiritual roots.

Fudarakusan-ji near the coast is a small temple of historical significance, associated with the cult of Kannon (bodhisattva of compassion). Kannon's island paradise, known as Mt Fudaraku, was said to lie in the south, and since Kumano is the southernmost point of Honshu, devotees felt drawn here. When abbots of the temple turned sixty, they set sail into the Pacific with petitions of their parishioners, never to return. Some twenty abbots perished in this way until the practice was banned after 1868. A model of the boat they used stands in the temple grounds.

BELOW The Nachi Waterfall is the largest in Japan, being 436 feet (133 meters) high and 43 feet (13 meters) wide. Large sutra mounds have been unearthed at the bottom, reflecting its popularity in medieval times when it was the object of worship for the Kumano Nachi/Seiganto-ji complex.

With its network of shrines and temples, Kumano was the biggest pilgrim destination of medieval Japan, drawing people of all classes. A network of routes developed that approached the Hongu Shrine from different directions, collectively known as Kumano Kodo (Kumano Old Roads). So popular was the pilgrimage that it gave rise to an expression about 'the ant trail to Kumano' since the narrow paths only allowed for single file. From Kyoto it took about 40 days to complete, and one emperor is said to have undertaken the pilgrimage 23 times accompanied by 1,000 retainers.

A whole support system developed to cater to pilgrims, including guides and accommodation. The toughest route was from Koyasan, with three mountain passes over 3,280 feet (1,000 meters) high. The most used route, however, ran along the west coast before cutting inland to the Kumano Hongu Shrine. From there, it was customary to travel to Hayatama Taisha by boat, now the only river pilgrimage to be registered as part of a World Heritage Site.

ABOVE LEFT Women pose in the medieval travel costume for high-class females, who would go on pilgrimage to the Kumano shrines. When encountering strangers, the long veil would be drawn over their faces.

ABOVE MIDDLE Along the Kumano Kodo are many monuments and stages for ascetic practice. It makes the landscape an important cultural as well as natural heritage.

ABOVE RIGHT Along the Omine Okugake route are some fine views of the Kii Peninsula mountain ranges. From ancient times, mountains have played a vital role in Japan's religious composition as the abode of the gods in which to undertake ascetic practice in order to gain spiritual merit.

RIGHT The Hayatama Grand Shrine in Shingu displays the characteristic Kumano style in its red and white coloring. Note, too, the *chigi* and *katsuogi* beams on the roof of the main structures.

Along the routes were stone markers, resting spots and small Oji shrines. There were also hot springs, notably Tsuboyu in the town of Yunomine near Hongu. Little more than a hut over a creek, it was used by medieval pilgrims for purification rites and the healing of sore limbs. This is the only UNESCO listed hot spring open to the public—a rare chance indeed to literally 'soak in' the atmosphere of a World Heritage Site.

YOSHINO AND OMINE

AN OLD PILGRIMAGE ROUTE CONNECTING TEMPLES AND SHRINES DEDICATED TO MOUNTAIN ASCETICISM

Yoshino and Omine lie either side of the Kii Mountains. Both are associated with Japan's mountain asceticism (Shugendo), and it's said that the founder, En no Gyoja, practised here in the seventh century. Shugendo draws on elements from Buddhism and Shinto, based on the notion that by performing austerities in a mountain setting practitioners enhance their spirituality.

Mt Yoshino holds a special place in Japanese hearts for its historic associations and cherry blossom (30,000 trees). The small town is dominated by Kinpusen-ji, a Shugendo temple of massive proportions. Last rebuilt in 1592, the Zao-do is Japan's second biggest wooden hall after Nara's Todai-ji. The magnificent sculptures portray Zao

Gongen, deity of mountain asceticism.

Yoshimizu Shrine, a short walk away, has the air of an aristocratic villa. The twelfth-century warrior Yoshitsune used it as a refuge, Emperor Godaigo stayed during the Southern Court period, and Hideyoshi came for the cherry blossom. Formerly a part of Kinpusen-ji, it now exhibits art work and offers fine views.

Further up the hill lies Yoshino Mikumari Shrine, which originated with water worship. Reconstructed in 1605, it has a long Worship Hall facing a row of sanctuaries. At the top of the hill is the modest Kinpu Shrine, dedicated to the spirit of place. Its *torii* is an important gateway in the ritual of 'entering the mountains'. (From the Yoshino ropeway 90 minutes walk or 20 minutes by bus.)

RIGHT Kinpusen-ji in Yoshino contains a statue of Zao Gongen, deity of mountain asceticism, supposedly carved by En no Gyoja from a cherry tree. Thereafter, cherry trees were cherished as sacred, and today the area has some 30,000 in all.

The Okugakemichi pilgrimage route, which continues from the Yoshino hill as far as Kumano Hongu, passes along ridges more than 3,280 feet (1,000 meters) high. Along the way are some 75 places for ascetic practice. The terrain is severe, but Shugendo practitioners are required to complete the course, and a video at the Yoshino Visitors Center shows initiates being dangled over a cliff edge on Mt Omine. The sacred mountain, which is closed to women, has a temple at the top constructed in 1691, with low eaves and thick pillars.

At the southern end of the Omine Mountains is the remote Tamaki Shrine, which is the protective shrine of the Totsukawa area. It is dedicated to the deity of gems, rocks and minerals. It's one of several staging posts along the route for Shugendo practitioners, and accommodation facilities were first put in during the Kamakura era. The shrine boasts 3,000-year-old cedar trees and is a fine exemplar of the continuing role of mountain worship in Japan's religious tradition.

ABOVE Yoshimizu Shrine, once part of Kinpusen-ji, has some precious paintings as well as associations with famous figures from Japan's past.

LEFT Mt Omine, known also as Sanjogatake, has a gateway beyond which it is forbidden for women to pass. Such prohibitions were once common on sacred mountains, although only here is it still practised.

WORLD HERITAGE SITES OF HIRAIZUMI

Remains of Japan's Former 'Northern Capital'

REGISTRATION 2011, as 'Hiraizumi—Temples, Gardens and Archaeological Sites Representing the Buddhist Pure Land'.

FEATURES Five components: Chuson-ji and Motsu-ji Temples, Kanjizaio-in and Muryoko-in remains and sacred hill of Kinkeisan.

ACCESS From Tokyo, JR train to Hiraizumi stn (2 hrs 10 mins). From the station a Loop Bus runs every 30 mins round the properties (Y400 all-day ticket). Bicycle rental at the station.

INFORMATION JR Hiraizumi Tourist Information Office: Tel. (0191) 46-2110; fax (0191) 46-2117. Exhibition at Hiraizumi Cultural Heritage Center. Goodwill Guides (free): o.kazuaki@nexyzbb.ne.jp.

OTHER ATTRACTIONS Takkoku no Iwaya cliff temple and Yanaginogosho (remains of former government buildings) are part of a proposal to extend the Hiraizumi World Heritage Site. Also of interest is a memorial (Takadachi Gikeido) to the twelfth-century warrior Yoshitsune.

In the twelfth century, Hiraizumi rivaled Kyoto for splendor and was known as 'the northern capital'. Temple complexes and aristocratic villas were set around landscaped gardens, which spoke of salvation in Amida's Pure Land (paradise). The cultural flowering owed itself to the Northern branch of the country's most powerful family, the Fujiwara, who had established Hiraizumi as their base.

Thanks to the region's production of gold, the Fujiwara were able to fund construction of a sacred city. Fujiwara no Kiyohira established Chuson-ji, his son Motohira founded Motsu-ji, and his grandson Hidehira sponsored Muryoko-in. Thousands of cherry trees were planted and sutras buried on the holy hill of Kinkeisan.

In 1189, the city was razed by Minamoto Yoritomo, soon to be the country's first shogun, and major fires subsequently furthered the decline. The elements that survived offer today a tantalising glimpse of the former glory—a vision of paradise on earth.

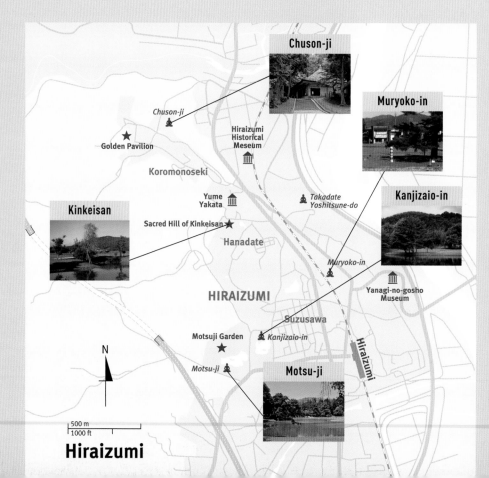

Hiraizumi

CHUSON-JI
A TRANQUIL MEMORIAL TO FALLEN HEIAN WARRIORS

BELOW The wooded approach to the temple leads past temple outbuildings, one of which is the Benkei Hall dedicated to the famed warrior-monk who died in Hiraizumi defending his master, Yoshitsune.

The glory days of Hiraizumi began when Fujiwara no Kiyohira settled there at the end of the eleventh century and commissioned a temple for the souls of those who had died in recent fighting. Although a successful warrior, he was moved to pursue peace by the death of his closest family members. Unusually, his temple was dedicated to all who had fallen, whether friend or foe, human or animal. Inspired by the Pure Land of Amida, he sought to build a fitting memorial.

The approach to Chuson-ji leads up an incline along a wooded path. The Hondo (Main Hall) is a relatively modern building, with a training area for sutra copying and meditation. A little further along is a complex of buildings, amongst which is the Sankozo Museum housing some 3,000 items, including the complete Buddhist canon written on blue paper in gold and silver, which took eight years and comprises 5,300 scrolls.

The jewel in the temple's crown is the Konjikido (Golden Hall), built in 1124 and acclaimed as one of the world's most beautiful buildings. The entire room is covered in gold leaf, augmented by mother-of-pearl inlay, gold-sprinkled lacquer and gilt-bronze plaques. The central object of worship is Amida, and below the dais are kept the mummified remains of four Fujiwara patriarchs. 'Early summer rains/fall not here/temple of light,' wrote poet Matsuo Basho.

So delicate was the Konjikido that it needed protection, and a Former Shelter Hall stands in the grounds, replaced in 1968 by a fire-resistant structure. The temple's only other twelfth-century structure is the plain wooden Kyozo (Sutra Repository). Nearby Hakusan Shrine, formerly part of the temple complex, has a prized Noh stage where priests perform, but it's the dazzling Konjikido that lingers in the mind, as it did during the time of Marco Polo, for it is thought to have prompted his famous description of Japan as a land with roofs of gold.

LEFT The principal object of worship in the Main Hall (Hondo) is a statue of Shaka Nyorai, the historical Buddha. Monthly memorials are held here for the four generations of Fujiwara lords who established Hiraizumi.

ABOVE Though the Konjikido is an independent building, it is so precious and delicate that it has to be shielded from the elements by a protective shelter made of fire-resistant concrete.

BELOW The Tsukimizaka (Moon Viewing Slope) leading to Chuson-ji is lined with ancient cryptomeria. The trees were planted over 300 years ago by the Date clan, which sought to preserve the area.

MOTSU-JI

AN ANCIENT MONASTIC CENTER AND POND GARDEN

Motsu-ji once hosted a monastic complex comprising more than forty halls and stupas. Sponsored by the second Fujiwara lord, Motohira, it was said to be the finest in Japan, with residential quarters for 500 priests and huge boulevards lined with storehouses. Little remains now but earthworks and foundation stones. Fire ravaged the buildings in 1226, and by the seventeenth century the complex was largely overgrown, moving the poet Matsuo Basho to write:

> *The summer grasses*
> *Are all that is left behind*
> *Of warrior dreams.*

Somehow the pond garden, often referred to as a paradise garden, survived and is considered the best-preserved of its age. It is much admired for the techniques involved. Set against a backdrop of Mt Toyama, it incorporates the surrounding landscape into its design. The pond has a small island, a rocky cape and a gently curving beach, whilst the feeder stream mimics the winding contours of a river. In this way, the garden represents a microcosm of the Japanese landscape, with the 1,640-foot (500-meter)-long path offering fresh perspectives as the visitor moves around it.

BELOW The Motsu-ji Temple buildings are relatively modern since the site was for long neglected after the original buildings burnt down. The lavishly decorated main hall was said to have been more gorgeous than any of the Kyoto temples.

Pure Land gardens drew on Buddhist concepts imported from the continent, together with indigenous animist notions concerning harmonisation with nature. Immersion in the elegantly created scenery was thought to draw the devotee closer to the Pure Land of Utmost Bliss as promised by the savior Amida. Spirituality was written into the very fabric of the garden, for it was designed to elevate the mind as much as please the eye.

Around the lake are markers to indicate the site of former buildings, some of which were magnificent structures. The present temple dates from a later age, with the Jogyodo Hall (Circumambulation Hall) dating from 1732. Its oldest building, the Kaizando, commemorates the Fujiwara benefactors, and a Cultural Assets Repository contains the temple's treasures. But it is the pond garden that makes this site so special. More than a recreation of the Pure Land, it is the apogee of an art form.

ABOVE The feeder stream for the pond, constructed to look like a river running between rocks, is the scene every May for a re-enactment of Heian-era poetry contests when participants in traditional attire compose verses as saké cups are floated downstream.

BELOW The pond garden was a representation of Amida's Pure Land or Paradise. Around it were once arranged magnificent temple halls offering views of the landscaped surrounds, amongst which were a gently curving beach, a promontory and an islet.

HIRAIZUMI REMAINS AND MOUNT KINKEISAN

A SACRED HILL WITH SURROUNDING REMNANTS OF HEIAN SPLENDOR

HIRAIZUMI REMAINS AT A GLANCE

FEATURES 3 properties: Mt Kinkeisan together with temple remains at Kanjizaio-in and Muryoko-in. (Other remains such as those at Yanaginogosho have been nominated for inscription.)

ACCESS All sites are near the Loop Bus route. Kanzaio-in is adjacent to Motsu-ji, Muryoko-in has its own stop, and Kinkeisan is a 10 mins walk from Hiraizumi Cultural Center.

PRACTICALITIES All sites free of charge. Tourist Information (0191) 46-2110. Allow up to 30 mins at each site.

BELOW A pair of golden chickens are said to be buried on the peak of Kinkeisan (Golden Cockerel Hill), signifying its protective role in the Pure Land geography of ancient Hiraizumi. Each generation of Fujiwara lords also had Buddhist sutras buried there.

When Fujiwara Motohira founded **Motsu-ji**, he built a residence next door which was converted into the temple of Kanjizaio-in after his death. Like its neighbor, it centered around a Pure Land pond garden, though more modest in size. The temple was destroyed by fire in 1226 but the pond remains in a park open to the public. The location of a Small and Large Amida Hall are marked, and it is thought that Motohira's widow lived in one and worshipped at the other.

Muryoko-in was the third of the great temple complexes at Hiraizumi, modeled on Byodo-in near Kyoto. Its main hall stood on a small island, as if floating on water. Now, little remains but foundation stones and garden traces aligned towards Hiraizumi's holy hill, Kinkeisan. Twice a year, at the equinoxes, the sun sets directly behind the mountain—symbolic for worshippers, as west was the location of Amida's Pure Land.

ABOVE Excavations at Yanaginogoshi suggest that the site was once the administrative center of Hiraizumi. Tradition also claims it is where the first and second Fujiwara lords had their palaces. The area is being carefully restored and a nearby museum displays artifacts.

LEFT The garden of the former temple of Kanjizaio-in is centered around the Maizurugaike or Dancing Crane Pond. Until recent times, rice fields covered the area, but after restoration it has been made into a public park.

A ten-minute walk away lie the remains of Yanaginogosho, thought to have been Hiraizumi's administrative center. In the 1980s, when a major bypass was planned, excavations turned up twelfth-century artifacts which are housed at a nearby museum. The site now has a pleasant park and recreated pond, with noticeboards to indicate the location of former buildings.

The small hill of Kinkeisan (322 feet/ 98 meters tall) lay at the center of the twelfth-century estates, and legend tells how a golden hen and rooster were placed at the summit as protectors of the city. Each generation of Fujiwara lords buried precious sutra scrolls on the hill, making it a spiritual as well as physical focus. When the poet Matsuo Basho visited Hiraizumi, he was moved by the ruins of the town and noted that 'Only Kinkeisan retains its shape.' Now, it stands some-what forlorn, with only the simplest of shrines at the top. Standing there, one can't help but wonder at how this most modest of spots once spoke of salvation—a holy hill in a sacred city.

WORLD HERITAGE SITES OF NIKKO

Magnificent Mausoleums of the Tokugawa Shoguns

REGISTRATION In 1999, as 'Shrines and Temples of Nikko'.

FEATURES Two Shinto shrines and a Buddhist temple in 125 acres (50 hectares) of wooded slopes: Tosho-gu, Futarasan Shrine and Rinno-ji.

ACCESS From Tokyo to Tobu Nikko or JR Nikko (about 2 hours), then 30 mins by foot or 10 mins by bus.

PRACTICALITIES Y1000 combination ticket. Tourist Information (0288) 54-2496. Volunteer guide (apply in advance): wisteriayoshiko@yahoo.co.jp / nm04954@nifty.com.

DATELINE
766—Shodo Shonin founds a temple
  (origin of Rinno-ji)
c. 790—Shodo Shonin founds a shrine
  (origin of Futarasan)
1617—Tosho-gu (mausoleum of Tokugawa
  Ieyasu)
1636—Enlargement by his grandson
  Tokugawa Iemitsu
1653—Taiyu-in (mausoleum for Iemitsu)
  built at Rinno-ji

Nikko is one of Japan's most popular tourist destinations; 'Don't say magnificent until you've been to Nikko,' runs a well-known saying. The World Heritage Site consists of 103 buildings in all, together with their woodland setting, and taken as a whole they reflect the wide range of traditional aesthetics. In the past, they would have represented a unified complex, but following the Meiji Restoration of 1868 the new government divided it into separate parts.

The area around Nikko has been sacred since ancient times, but it was only in 1617 that it came to national prominence after being chosen as the final resting place of the shogun Tokugawa Ieyasu. His mausoleum was so splendid that it became a place of wide renown, even overseas. Added to the attractions of the site is the nearby National Park, which features scenic landscapes, hot springs and hiking trails. The area is famous for its autumn colors, though a word of warning: at weekends and holidays you certainly won't be alone!

Nikko

500 m
1000 ft

N

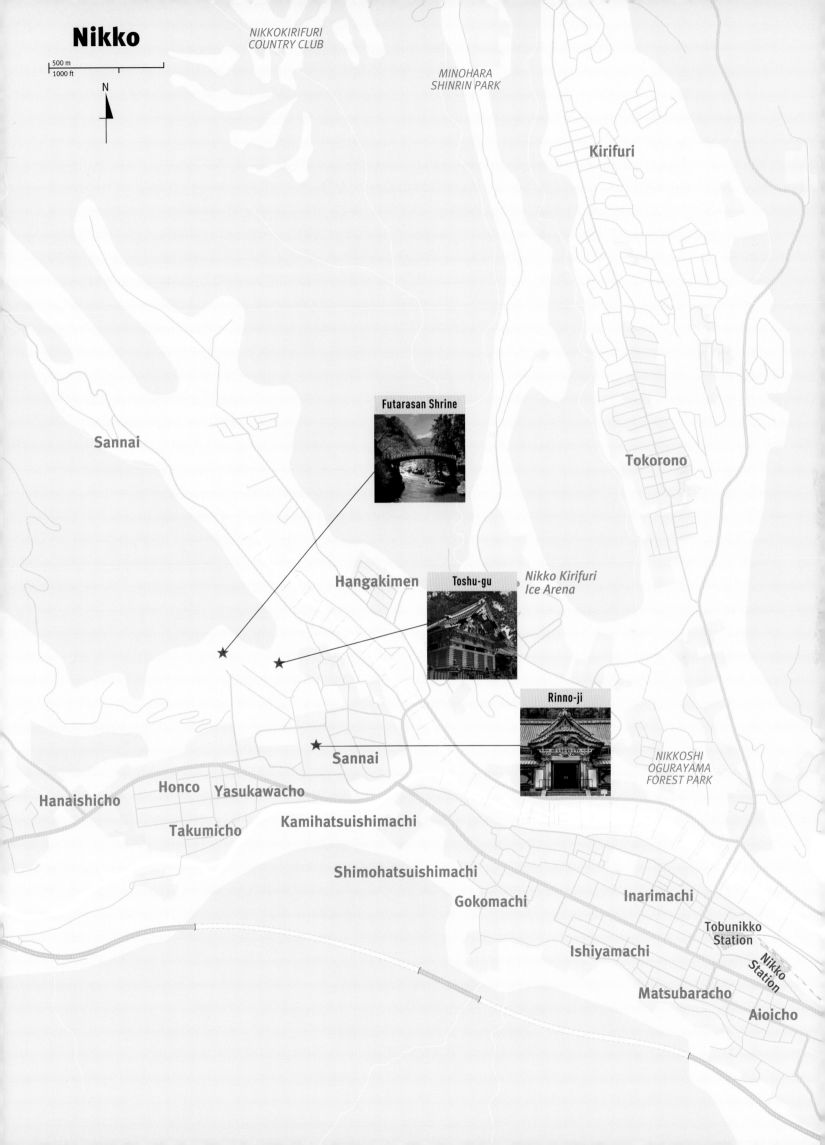

NIKKOKIRIFURI
COUNTRY CLUB

MINOHARA
SHINRIN PARK

Kirifuri

Futarasan Shrine

Sannai

Tokorono

*Nikko Kirifuri
Ice Arena*

Hangakimen   **Toshu-gu**

Rinno-ji

Sannai

*NIKKOSHI
OGURAYAMA
FOREST PARK*

Honco   **Yasukawacho**

Hanaishicho

Takumicho   **Kamihatsuishimachi**

Shimohatsuishimachi

Gokomachi

Inarimachi

Tobunikko
Station

Nikko
Station

Ishiyamachi

Matsubaracho

Aioicho

TOSHO-GU

THE SUMPTUOUS MEMORIAL TO JAPAN'S FIRST SHOGUN

TOSHO-GU AT A GLANCE

FEATURES 42 buildings and Tokugawa Ieyasu's grave. Amongst the lavish decorations are some famous carvings.

ACCESS From the Nikko train stations, about 30 mins walk or by bus. The shrine lies between Futarasan Shrine and Rinno-ji Temple.

PRACTICALITIES 8.00–17.00/16.00 (winter). Y1300 for all parts (Y1000 for shrine; Y520 for Ieyasu's tomb). Shrine tel. (0288) 54-0560. Allow 1 hour or more.

EVENTS Major festivals are held on May 17/18 and Oct 17/18.

FOUNDED 1617; reconstructed in 1636.

BELOW Tosho-gu sits on the slope of a hill, necessitating several flights of stairs. Here the steps lead up to the Niomon entrance gate with its fearsome Deva King guardians.

Amazing, stunning, overwhelming—reactions to Tosho-gu are often extreme because of the lavish decoration. Brightly colored and covered with carvings, the shrine is the ultimate contrast with Japan's traditional taste for modesty and simplicity. It represents a display of power by the most successful shogunate dynasty in Japanese history, the Tokugawa. The family ruled the country from 1600 to 1867. The vivid colors of the shrine reflect the Chinese influence of a regime whose ideology rested on Neo-Confucianism.

Enshrined at Tosho-gu is the dynasty's founding father, Tokugawa Ieyasu (1543–1616). Before he died, Ieyasu expressed his desire to be laid to rest at Nikko, from where his spirit would look down on the nation to ensure its well-being. In 1617, a mausoleum was built in his honor by his son Hidetada, and he was duly deified and given the

RIGHT The Sanjinko are three adjacent storehouses in which are kept the 1,200 costumes used in the Sennin Musha Procession as well as equipment for the shrine's *yabusame* horse archery.

BELOW The lavishly carved Yomeimon has, in the words of UNESCO, 'a profusion and infinite variety of decoration'. It has been described as a Wonderland, with over 500 sculptures, including exotic animals like giraffes and mythical animals such as horse-dragons.

posthumous name of Tosho Daigongen (Great Avatar of the Shining East).

Nearly twenty years later, Ieyasu's grandson Iemitsu determined to build a grander memorial to show the extent of his reverence. Accordingly, he carried out substantial rebuilding, which involved the addition of elaborate decorations. Altogether, some 1,500 workers were employed to work on the project, which was completed for the twentieth anniversary of Ieyasu's death. It was not only a powerful statement of shogunate power but an assertion of the family's divine right to rule. As such, it became a site of pilgrimage for Tokugawa loyalists and a place to pay respects for foreign dignitaries.

The shrine stands on a wooded slope, necessitating several flights of stairs as one ascends up through the shrine to Ieyasu's grave, the 'holy of holies'. The approach to the shrine is marked by one of the largest stone *torii* in Japan, ingeniously constructed so as to be resistant to earthquakes; joints in the crossbeam allow for movement. Beyond it stands a five-storey pagoda and a gate with guardian Nio (Deva Kings), Buddhist elements at the shrine which somehow managed to survive the forced separation of Shinto and Buddhism in the late nineteenth century.

Within the shrine buildings are some famous structures, none more so than the Yomeimon Gate with its richly colored carvings in deep relief. It's been dubbed the Gate of Dusk (Higurashi no mon) because one can stand and gaze at it all day long. There are over 500 sculpted pieces depicting flowers, animals, patterns and people from moral tales. If one looks hard enough, it becomes apparent that one of the twelve white pillars of the gate has been inverted, which is a deliberate flaw in order to suggest incompleteness, for the work has not yet been perfected.

Amongst the shrine's lavish decorations are some striking animal carvings. There is an almost comical depiction of an elephant, for example, by someone who

ABOVE The guardian archers or *zuijin* who sit at the foot of the Yomeimon Gate derive originally from the Heian-era bodyguards of the emperor.

BELOW LEFT Men dressed in samurai uniform take part in the shrine's festival, re-enacting the removal of Ieyasu's spirit to Nikko from its temporary abode at Mt Kuno. Members of the Tokugawa family attend, and among the ceremonies are dance and horse performances.

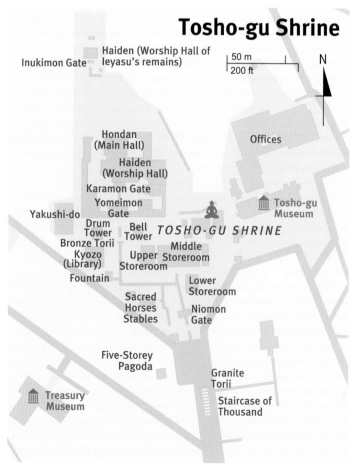

Tosho-gu Shrine

Inukimon Gate · Haiden (Worship Hall of Ieyasu's remains)

50 m / 200 ft

N

Hondan (Main Hall)

Offices

Haiden (Worship Hall)

Karamon Gate

Yomeimon Gate

Yakushi-do

Tosho-gu Museum

Drum Tower · Bell Tower · *TOSHO-GU SHRINE*

Bronze Torii

Kyozo (Library) · Middle Storeroom

Upper Storeroom

Fountain

Lower Storeroom

Sacred Horses Stables · Niomon Gate

Five-Storey Pagoda

Granite Torii

Treasury Museum

Staircase of Thousand

had clearly never seen a real one. More celebrated, however, is a Sleeping Cat above the entrance leading to Ieyasu's grave, which has been interpreted in different ways. Some think that it protects his remains from rats, but the nearby carvings of sparrows at play suggest that the intention was rather to show the benefits of peace and a warning not to provoke the 'Tokugawa cat'.

The most famous of the carvings appears on the Stables where the sacred white mount of the *kami* is kept. A series of eight sculpted panels depicts the life cycle of monkeys, including the renowned 'See no evil, hear no evil, speak no evil.' Although they were meant to be a simple moral instruction, the Three Wise Monkeys became reinterpreted in the West as a warning against compliance with evil, an interesting example of how stories take on new meanings as they travel.

To the east of the shrine is an avenue of trees, about 12 miles (20 km) long, which is certified as the longest in the world. Lined with over 13,000 cedars, it was part of an extensive plantation carried out by a Tokugawa ally in the early seventeenth century. Such was the status of Tosho-gu that it attracted huge shogunal processions to honor the spirit of the dynastic founder, who was cast as father of a peaceful nation. The great processions of the past are recalled in Nikko's biannual festival, when participants in Edo-era costume re-enact the original parade which bore Ieyasu's remains to the site. Should you happen to be in Nikko on such days, you may well be moved to say 'magnificent' indeed.

ABOVE The five-storey pagoda was rebuilt in 1818 after being burnt down. It is 118 feet (36 meters) tall and inside is a huge pillar suspended from the fourth floor as a measure against earthquakes.

LEFT The Three Wise Monkeys originated in China but were popularised in the West through their representation at Tosho-gu. Carved by master-sculptor Hidari Jingoro, they are part of a series of eight panels showing Confucian ethics.

FUTARASAN SHRINE

A SHRINE DEDICATED TO NIKKO'S THREE SACRED MOUNTAINS

**FUTARASAN SHRINE
AT A GLANCE**

FEATURES A Shinto shrine with 23 structures, including Shinkyo Bridge.

ACCESS From the Nikko train stations, about 30 mins walk or just over 600 feet (200 meters) west of Tosho-gu.

PRACTICALITIES 8.00–17.00. Shrine free, Y200 for precincts. Shrine tel. (0288) 54-0535; fax (0288) 54-0537. Allow up to 1 hour.

FOUNDATION Antecedent founded c. 790 by Shodo Shonin.

OPPOSITE TOP The Worship Hall (Haiden), with its distinctive curving roof, became a model for the style of later shrines.

BELOW The pathway to the Futarasan Shrine is lined with stone lanterns and woodland, exemplifying the harmony with nature in UNESCO's World Heritage Site citation.

Futarasan may be overshadowed by Tosho-gu but it is a shrine of interest in its own right. Founded by a Buddhist monk, it is not only representative of Japan's syncretism but of its nature worship, for enshrined here are the personified spirits of three local mountains: Mt Nantai, Mt Nyoho and Mt Taro. The greatest of the three, at 8,000 feet (2,438 meters), is the Fuji-shaped volcano Mt Nantai (also called Futarasan). In ancient times, the waters that flowed from the mountain peaks, which were vital to wet-rice cultivation, were ascribed to the benevolence of the *kami* who lived on the upper slopes.

The most famous of the shrine's structures stands at the Daiya River, where the rainbow-arched Shinkyo Bridge once formed the official entrance.

Tradition says that when Shodo Shonin was unable to cross the river a water deity ordered two snakes to form a crossing. The bridge took its present shape in the seventeenth century when it was reserved for imperial messengers. Nowadays, it is open to the public (for a small fee) and is a popular place for wedding photos.

The Worship Hall (Haiden) of Futarasan was built around 1644 in a simple, undecorated style, which became a model for later shrines. The precincts, for which an extra charge is made, include a number of unusual features, such as representations of the shrine's three sacred mountains. There's a Hall of Daikoku, deity of good fortune, outside of which a fortune-telling game can be played, and there's also a copper 'ghost lantern' whose flickering flames were so unnerving that guards lashed out at them with their swords; the cuts are still evident.

At the back of the sanctuary is a holy spring (Reisen) said to protect against eye disease. The water is so pure that it is used for saké making, and a teahouse offers the opportunity to try some in a cup of whipped green tea. The taste, you could say, is divine.

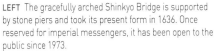

LEFT The gracefully arched Shinkyo Bridge is supported by stone piers and took its present form in 1636. Once reserved for imperial messengers, it has been open to the public since 1973.

BELOW Within the entrance gate at the beginning of July are Tanabata decorations and a *chinowa* (circle of wreaths), through which visitors step for protection.

BOTTOM The Reisen Spring, containing sacred water, issues from a cave behind the Honden (Sanctuary) and was used for saké brewing and to protect against eye disease.

RINNO-JI

MAUSOLEUM OF THE THIRD SHOGUN IN THE TOKUGAWA LINE

**RINNO-JI
AT A GLANCE**

FEATURES A Tendai temple of 15 buildings, including Sanbutsudo (Three Buddhas Hall), Shoyoen Garden, Houmotsuden
(Treasure House) and Taiyu-in (mausoleum
of Tokugawa Iemitsu).

ACCESS From the Nikko train stations,
about 30 mins walk or by bus. The temple
lies on the east side of Tosho-gu.

PRACTICALITIES 8.00–17.00/16.00 (winter).
Y700. Tel. (0288) 54-0531; fax (0288) 54-0534.
Allow about 1 hour.

FOUNDATION Temple predecessor founded
in 766 by Shodo Shonin.

ABOVE RIGHT Looking out through the Rinno-ji entrance
gate shows how immersed the Nikko institutions are in
the surrounding woods.

BELOW Detail of a guardian creature on the lavishly
decorated Taiyu-in, built as a subtemple and mausoleum
for Tokugawa Iemitsu.

**Rinno-ji traces its origins to the eighth-
century monk Shodo Shonin**, who was
struck by the inspirational mountain
setting. The fortunes of the temple have
fluctuated over the centuries, but at
one time it was a flourishing center for
mountain asceticism. Rinno-ji rose to
national prominence in 1653 when a
mausoleum for Tokugawa Iemitsu

(1604–51) was added, following which it
formed the heart of a sprawling Shinto-
Buddhist complex. After the Meiji
Restoration of 1868, however, it was
stripped of its Shinto connections and
today has just fifteen buildings.

The main hall, Sanbutsudo, was
constructed in 1647 and moved to its
present site in 1879. It contains three
huge gold-lacquered statues, made
of wood. In the center stands Amida
Nyorai flanked by two attendants, the
1,000-headed Kannon and the Horse-
headed Kannon. In Shinto-Buddhist
syncretism, the triad equate to the three
mountain *kami* enshrined at Futarasan.

OPPOSITE ABOVE The Koukamon Gate, not open to the
public, leads to the grave of Iemitsu. It is one of several
heavily decorated gateways in the Taiyu-in complex.

OPPOSITE BELOW The massive Sanbutsudo (Three
Buddhas Hall) is Rinno-ji's prime place of worship. It
contains three huge gilded statues of Buddhist deities
representing the three sacred mountains of Nikko.
Major renovation of the hall is ongoing and scheduled
to last until 2021.

OPPOSITE ABOVE The Yashamon is also known as the Peony Gate after one of its motifs. It houses four guardian figures, each in a different color according to the direction they protect.

OPPOSITE BELOW Everything at Taiyu-in bears the hallmark of Tokugawa opulence, including this water basin for cleansing hands prior to entering.

ABOVE Though Iemitsu said his mausoleum should not be more gorgeous than his grandfather's, the highly decorated Karamon (Chinese-style gate) is impressive. Above the opening is a white dragon on golden waves.

RIGHT The pathway of the attractive Shoyoen garden leads the visitor around a central pond and through recreations of differing landscapes.

FAR RIGHT Smoke from the incense burning before Buddhist temples is thought to have protective qualities, and worshippers at Rinno-ji can often be seen wafting it over themselves.

Opposite the hall stands the temple's Treasure House containing valuable items, such as eighth-century scrolls. Next to it lies a Japanese pond garden called the Shoyoen, with mossy rocks and winding pathways in an enclosed haven of greenery. The layout is said to be based on Lake Biwa and exemplifies the Japanese genius for representation through reduction.

The Taiyu-in Mausoleum nearby comprises a small group of structures, with a striking Nio entrance gate. As grandson of the dynasty's founder, Iemitsu saw his predecessor in godlike terms and said, 'I will serve Ieyasu even after death.' His mausoleum faces that of his grandfather and is designed to harmonise with it while being slightly smaller. The overall effect is similarly dazzling, and as at Tosho-gu the vivid colors reflect the Chinese influence of a regime whose ideology rested on Neo-Confucianism. Even in death the intention was plain: the Tokugawa had a mandate from Heaven.

IWAMI SILVER MINE

A WELL-PRESERVED SIXTEENTH-CENTURY MINING DISTRICT

IWAMI SILVER MINE AT A GLANCE

REGISTRATION 2007, as 'Iwami Ginzan Silver Mine and Its Cultural Landscape'.

FEATURES Remains of Japan's largest silver mine, which functioned from 1526 to 1923. Three parts: mining area, Omori district and the trading routes to the small ports of Tomogaura, Okidomari and Yunotsu.

ACCESS From Osaka or Kyoto, JR train to Oda City in Shimane Prefecture, then 20 mins by bus to the Omori district. Alternatively, a day's side trip by bus from Hiroshima shinkansen exit (dep. 10.00, arr. 12.30).

INFORMATION Oda City Tourist Association (0854) 89-9090. World Heritage Center (0854) 89-0183. Goodwill guides (free; book in advance) tel//fax (0852) 27-2503. Rental bikes available; also an excellent audio guide for Y500.

DURATION Up to 5 hours to walk around the mining area and Omori town. Hiking and/or hot springs may require an overnight stay.

ATTRACTIONS Okubo and Ryugenji mine shafts, exhibitions at the World Heritage Center and Daikansho (Former Magistrate's Office), Kumagai Merchant's House, samurai house, Buddhist and Shinto sites, hiking trails to mountain forts and ports, hot springs.

RIGHT Only two mine shafts are open to the public. One is the tunnel-like Ryugenji (Y400), which runs between two sides of a hill. The other is the more spectacular Okubo, the largest and longest operating shaft, which is only open to tour groups (Y3800) organised by the World Heritage Center.

Iwami Ginzan was not only Japan's leading silver mine in the late sixteenth and early seventeenth centuries but was of global significance. It was even marked on a map of the world produced in Europe. At the time, Japanese silver production made up a third of the world's total, half of which was produced at Iwami. Portuguese ships traded it for the Chinese goods they brought to Japan, and the Jesuit mission was able to flourish as a result.

The mine was first developed in 1526 by a merchant from Hakata, who noticed a glow from one of the hills. He invited a pair of Koreans to set up an advanced production method known as 'cupellation', by which crushed ore is mixed with a solvent to remove impurities. The method spread to Japan's other silver

RIGHT In the palatial Kumagai Merchant's House, the scales that formed the heart of the family business were a prized item. Miners perished early, but merchants thrived from the silver business.

BELOW The Omori settlement, which lies in a river valley near the mining area, acted as administrative center for the shogunate. Samurai, merchants and craftsmen lived here in close proximity to each other.

mines, transforming the country from
a net importer to a major exporter. In
its early days the mine was fought over
by rival warlords, and the remains of
hill forts surround the site, but with the
ascendancy of the Tokugawa after 1600
the area came under direct control of the
shogunate, which set up a security fence.

Mining was carried out with a hammer
and chisel, the only light being a simple
wick in a turtle shell. At its peak, the
mine involved 10,000 people and 150
villages. Conditions were harsh, with
poor ventilation, dusty air and back-
breaking loads carried along low passages. Few survived very long, and there
were celebrations for those who reached
their thirtieth birthday. Protective shrines
and Buddhist memorials can be found
throughout the area, the most famous
being the 500 arhat statues in a hilly
recess opposite the temple of Rakan-ji.

A 30-minute walk from the mining
area is the charming district of Omura,
where administrators, merchants and
craftsmen used to live. It retains some
of its Edo-era character, with houses
tastefully converted into cafes and
souvenir shops. There's a well-preserved
samurai house, the modest proportions
of which are dwarfed by the massive
Kumagai Merchant's House with its

thirty rooms. It shows just how profitable
the mining was for some.

Silver was transported on horseback
to the coast, where, guarded by small
fortresses, it was transferred onto boats.
The 4-mile (6.5-km) trail to Tomogaura
was superseded in the late sixteenth
century by the 7.5-mile (12-km) route to
Okidomari and Kunotsu. The latter has
hot springs still enjoyed today, while at
the harbors can be seen 'nose-ring rocks'
where trading vessels once moored.

ABOVE LEFT At the disused Okidomari Port stands Ebisu
Shrine, dedicated to safety at sea. Boarded up and
dilapidated, it serves as a reminder of the former shipping
trade's importance. From here huge amounts of silver
were transported to Hakata, and then abroad.

ABOVE A small settlement overlooks Tomogaura, which
before Okidomari was the main port for dispatching silver.
In the early sixteenth century, it was a bustling area with
administrators, customs officials and a fort to guard the
shipments.

Iwami Silver Mine

Some 600 shafts were dug during the four centuries of operation. Digging had to go ever deeper after the surface ore was used up, and eventually the work proved unprofitable. In 1923, the mine was forced to close altogether. The World Heritage Center portrays its history, with exhibits showing how the ore was mined and purified. The largest of the mine shafts was Okubo, which remained in continuous use throughout. It can be visited on a group tour, although it closes in winter when only the Ryugenji shaft, built in 1715, is open for inspection.

Following closure of the mine, the area fell into decay until a determined effort at conservation brought recognition of the site's significance. The awarding of World Heritage Site status resulted not only

from its global role and well-preserved remnants but from the environmental aspect; during its four centuries of operation, trees used for fuel were replaced by extensive replanting. As a result, the area is covered in mixed woodland, making the former mine more than just a place of historical importance but one that is attractive to walkers, hikers and nature lovers.

LEFT The mine area is covered with small openings, some of which defy belief that people could enter them for work. As well as damp, dark and dusty conditions, workers had to bend double to carry crippling loads of ore.

BELOW The Ryugenji mine shaft leads 190 feet (158 meters) into the mountain before connecting to a specially made exit tunnel. Built in 1715, it was mostly hollowed out by hand before the introduction of dynamite. In 1858, a total of 39 miners, including 10 year olds, worked here in two shifts.

WORLD HERITAGE SITES OF OKINAWA

Splendid Remains of the Former Ryukyu Empire

REGISTRATION 2000, as 'Gusuku Sites and Related Properties of the Kingdom of Ryukyu'.

FEATURES 5 castles (Shuri, Nakijin, Zakimi, Katsuren, Nakagusuku); 2 sacred sites (Sonohyan Gate, Seifa Utaki); 1 garden (Shikinaen); 1 mausoleum (Tamaudun)

ACCESS Within Naha, properties are accessible by public transport (Shuri Castle, Sonohyan, Tamaudun and Shikinaen). Others can be reached by bus but a car is recommended.

PRACTICALITIES Naha Tourist Information (098-868-4887). Allow 3 days to see everything.

DATELINE
1322–1429—Three Kingdoms (Sanzan)
1429—Ryukyu Kingdom formed by the Sho
1609—Control by Japan's Satsuma domain
1879—End of Ryukyu Kingdom and integration into Japan as Okinawa Prefecture

From 1429 to 1879 Okinawa was an independent country known as the Ryukyu Kingdom, which lay at the intersection of East Asian trading routes. It developed a distinctive culture that borrowed from neighboring countries, and this is reflected in its World Heritage Site properties. The showpiece is the restored Shuri Castle, the foundations of which are listed by UNESCO, close to which are the Sonohyan Shrine Stone Gate and the Tamaudun Mausoleum. A short taxi ride away is the Shikinaen Garden, which served as a royal villa.

The chief religious site of the Ryukyu Kingdom was Seifa Utaki, located in the southeast of the island. It consists of natural features, and the rites mixed animism and ancestor worship in a form unique to Okinawa. Today, the site still exudes a sense of the numinous.

The remaining properties are the fortification ruins of four Okinawan-style castles, known as *gusuku*, spread around the main island. Their construction dates from the twelfth to the fifteenth centuries, and though they stand in various states of ruin the solid walls speak of the struggle for unification and the subsequent years of peace. Here, in the stone remains, the Ryukyu heritage lives on.

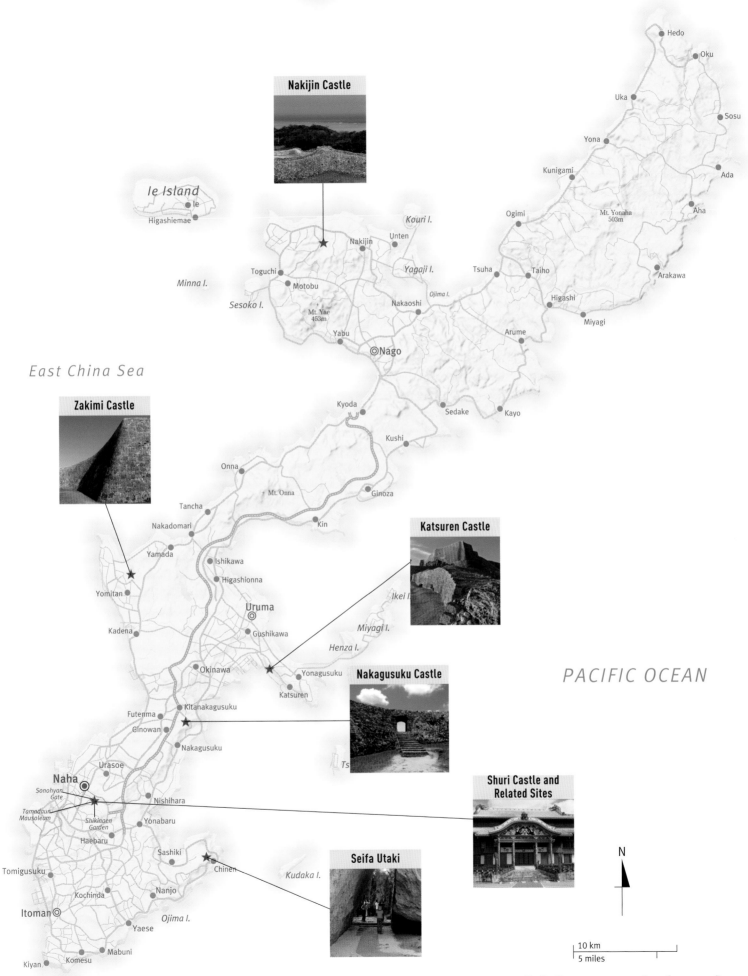

Nakijin Castle

Zakimi Castle

Katsuren Castle

Nakagusuku Castle

Shuri Castle and Related Sites

Seifa Utaki

Izena Island

Yanaha I.

Hedo
Oku
Uka
Sosu
Yona
Ada
Kunigami
Ogimi
Mt. Yonaha 503m
Aha
Tsuha
Taiho
Arakawa
Higashi
Miyagi
Arume

Kouri I.
Nakijin
Unten
Ie Island
Ie
Higashiemae
Yagaji I.
Toguchi
Motobu
Nakaoshi
Ojima I.
Minna I.
Mt. Yae 453m
Yabu
Sesoko I.
◎Nago

East China Sea

Kyoda
Sedake
Kayo
Kushi
Onna
Mt. Onna
Ginoza
Tancha
Nakadomari
Kin
Yamada
Ishikawa
Higashionna
Yomitan
Uruma
Kadena
Gushikawa
Ikei I.
Okinawa
Yonagusuku
Miyagi I.
Katsuren
Henza I.
Kitanakagusuku
Futenma
Ginowan
Nakagusuku
Urasoe
PACIFIC OCEAN
Naha ◎
Sonohyan Gate
Nishihara
Tamadaun Mausoleum
Shikinaen Garden
Yonabaru
Haebaru
Sashiki
Tomigusuku
Chinen
Kudaka I.
Kochinda
Nanjo
Itoman ◎
Ojima I.
Yaese
Mabuni
Kiyan
Komesu

10 km
5 miles

N

Okinawa Island

SHURI CASTLE AND RELATED SITES

THE RYUKYU PALACE WITH ITS ROYAL MAUSOLEUM, GATE AND GARDEN

SHURI CASTLE RELATED SITES AT A GLANCE

FEATURES Shuri Castle remains, Tamaudun Mausoleum, Sonohyan Stone Gate, Shikinaen Garden.

ACCESS From downtown Naha, bus to Shuri Castle (no.1 or 4), or by monorail then 20 mins walk. Sonohyan (1 min) and Tamaudun (10 mins) are close by. Shikinaen Garden is 20 mins by bus (no. 2, 5, 14).

PRACTICALITIES Castle 8.30–17.30/19.30 (seasonal). Y800. Sonohyan Gate free. Tamaudun Mausoleum 9.00–18.00. Y300. Shikinaen 9.00–18.00/17.30 (seasonal). Y400. Allow up to half a day for all.

INFORMATION Shuri Castle Park has an information center. Tel.(098) 886-2020. There are also souvenir shops and Okinawan food.

DATELINE
c. 1350—Shuri Castle founded
1501—Tamaudun established
1519—Sonohyan Gate erected
1799—Shikinaen laid out
1945—Shuri Castle destroyed
1992—Reconstruction begun

OPPOSITE ABOVE The graceful Shureimon, originally erected in the sixteenth century, was the first part of the castle to be reconstructed after the devastation of World War II. It bears the slogan 'Land of Propriety'.

OPPOSITE BELOW The reconstructed Seiden of Shuri Castle, with its eye-catching bright colors, is Okinawa's prime tourist sight. The architecture is a reminder of the Ryukyu Kingdom's mediating role between China and Japan.

Shuri Castle was the seat of Ryukyu power for some 450 years. It stands on a small hill, 394 feet (120 meters) above sea level, overlooking Naha city and port. It is here that the Ryukyu kings lived and here that important ceremonies of state were carried out. During World War II the castle was devastated, but a determination to rebuild it in the same form led to a painstaking reconstruction. Although the World Heritage Site listing applies to the original remains, the restored castle shows the form it would have taken. It is not only a reminder of a proud past but is the prefecture's prime tourist sight.

The castle was first built in the fourteenth century when it served as base for the Central Kingdom during the wars of unification. Afterwards it became the residence of the Ryukyu kings, serving also for state rituals. The sturdy walls, 33 feet (10 meters) high in places, enclose large ceremonial spaces, the first of which contains an *utaki* sacred shrine in the form of a sacred tree before which offerings were made.

The inner enclosure is fronted by the magnificent Seiden, the largest wooden structure in Okinawa. Here was the administrative and political heart of the realm. The building has a Japanese-style roof but shows Chinese influence in its vermilion lacquer and dragon patterns. Since Ryukyu was a seafaring nation, the kings adopted the watery dragon as their motif and the creature is everywhere evident. There are dragon figures decorating the interior, dragons on the roof and 13-foot (4-meter)-high dragon pillars on either side of the entrance.

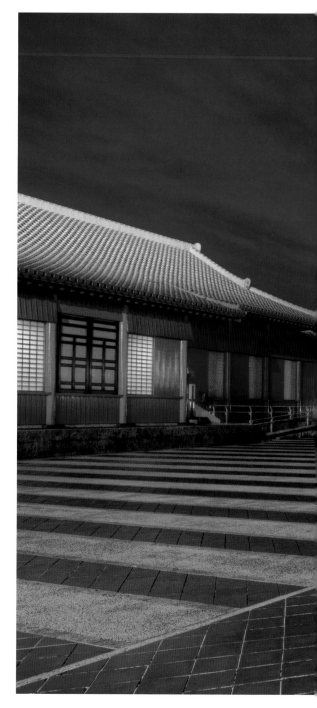

The first floor of the Seiden was used specifically for royal audiences and public affairs, while the second was reserved for rituals and female usage. The rooms opened onto the courtyard where Chinese envoys and other dignitaries would be received. Ryukyu craftsmanship was evident in the decor, which features lacquerware with gold inlay, mother-of-pearl and intricate carvings in bright colors.

On either side of the courtyard were two buildings for the affairs of state. The North Hall dealt with political matters, while the Southern was for the king's office, adjoining which a tearoom overlooked an Okinawan-style garden featuring local limestone and pine trees. Today, the Sasunoma Tea Room offers Ryukyu-style pastries.

Outside the castle exit is the Sonohyan Stone Gate, the style of which is peculiar to Okinawa. The doors were never opened, for behind the gate stood a sacred grove (*utaki*) which contained the tutelary spirit of the castle and by extension the country as a whole. The king would stop before the gate to offer prayers when entering or leaving the castle, and rituals were performed for the well-being of the nation.

Ten minutes away is the Tamaudun Mausoleum. A stone building with three chambers, it is carved into a limestone bedrock and holds the remains of eighteen kings. Ancestor worship is important to Okinawans, and the Sho kings wanted to boost their authority through the grandeur of the family tomb. The east chamber was for monarchs and consorts, the west for family members, and the center for the washing of bones in ritual manner. On the roof stand *shisa*

TOP The hill on which Shuri Castle stands dominates Naha City and its port. The enclosure walls, built with a bonding of coralline limestone, extend over 3,543 feet (1,080 meters).

ABOVE Behind the closed doors of the Sonohyan Stone Gate is a sacred grove (*utaki*), believed to house protective spirits. On departing their palace, Ryukyu kings stopped here to pray for a safe journey and gave thanks when returning.

OPPOSITE BELOW LEFT Surmounting the roof of the Seiden are guardian dragons, a symbol of the Ryukyu Kingdom which saw itself as a maritime nation.

lion-dog guardians characteristic of Okinawa and further evidence of Chinese cultural and architectural influence.

At the end of the eighteenth century, the Shikinaen Villa was established as a second royal residence. Although it was completely destroyed in World War II, it was restored over a twenty-year period from 1975. The focal point of the garden is a hexagonal building on a small island reached by an arched bridge made from a single block of stone. Around the pond are pavilions, artificial hills, flower gardens and a wooded area. Plants are arranged to show the change of seasons.

Although the pond garden is based on Japanese design, structures such as the bridge and gazebo show Chinese influence while walls made of local limestone lend an Okinawan flavor. The modesty of scale may reflect the limitations of the island country, sandwiched between two large imperial neighbors, but in the combinatory style can be sensed something quite distinctive, something special indeed to the Ryukyu Kingdom.

ABOVE LEFT Kankaimon, meaning Welcome Gate, is on the outer of the castle's double enclosures. A wooden turret sits above a stone arch, and on either side are protective stone *shisha* (lion-dogs).

ABOVE RIGHT The pond garden of the Shikinaen Royal Villa was laid out according to Japanese models, though many of the features show Chinese influence or reflect a local touch through the use of native limestone and coral.

BELOW The reconstructed Ryukyu throne on the second floor of the Seiden building was where the king presided over ceremonies, backed by a framed inscription from the Chinese emperor.

BOTTOM A replica of the crown once worn by Ryukyu kings is on display in the Seiden, one of several treasures to have been carefully restored to the destroyed palace.

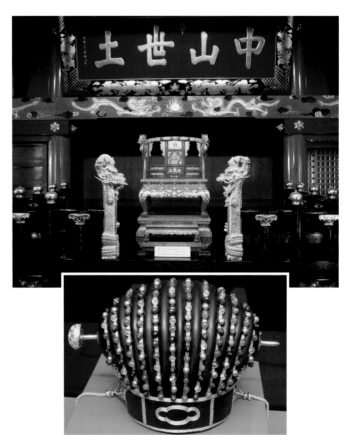

SEIFA UTAKI

THE RYUKYU KINGDOM'S SACRED SPIRITUAL SITE

**SEIFA UTAKI
AT A GLANCE**

FEATURE A wooded hillside with cliff and rock face.

ACCESS From Naha terminal, take bus no. 38 to Seifa-Utaki-mae (about 60 mins, Y810).

PRACTICALITIES 9.00–17.30. Y200. Brochure in English, audio guide available. Nanjo City Tourist Information tel. 098-949-1899. Allow up to 1 hour.

DATELINE
1429—High priestesses (Kikoe Okimi) appointed following Ryukyu unification
1879—Site's official role ends with abolition of Ryukyu Kingdom

During the time of the Ryukyu Kingdom, Seifa Utaki was the seat of spiritual authority with close ties to royalty. (*Seifa* means 'supreme' and *utaki* is a 'sacred place'.) The site's high priestess was linked to the king through blood ties, and the ceremonial areas were named after rooms at the royal palace. Amongst the ceremonies performed were important rites of state, for which royal visitors would arrive by boat. Viewed in historical terms, this simple hillside was the nation's 'cathedral' as fashioned by nature.

No men were allowed into the site, as Okinawan tradition delegated all religious duties to women. Before the entrance is a spring where priestesses would purify themselves, then the path runs through subtropical woodland to a cliffside 'main hall', in front of which rituals were performed. Thereafter, a fork in the path leads to a 'kitchen', where food offerings were prepared in a rocky recess.

At the end of the main pathway is the site's most sacred area, comprising a triangular opening in a rock face. Before the entrance are placed two pots beneath a pair of stalactites, from which drips water that is used for rituals and divination. On the other side of the opening is a small ceremonial area with a view of Kudaku Island, which features in the

OPPOSITE The most sacred part of Seifa Utaki lies through a triangular opening. On the far side a view opens up of Kudaku Island, mythical origin of Okinawa, and there are simple altars once used by high priestesses.

TOP Holy water, collected from two stalactites to the right of the triangular opening, was used for divination and consecration.

ABOVE Markers indicating the site's World Heritage status stand close to the entrance, beyond which only members of the royal family could pass. Ordinary people worshipped outside, before symbolic incense burners.

RIGHT Food was prepared on the stone platform for offering to the gods, as a result of which the area was referred to with the same name (Yuinchi) as the kitchen in the royal palace at Shuri Castle.

nation's Creation Myth. According to tradition, it was here that the gods first landed when settling Okinawa.

In the early morning or late afternoon, when visitors are few, it is easy to imagine how awe-inspiring Seifa Utaki must once have been. Even today it remains a sacred site, and to preserve its sanctity it is closed to the public for certain days to allow for worship. The Ryukyu Kingdom no longer exists, but the animism that it cherished lives on in these very special surroundings.

ANCIENT RYUKYU CASTLES
THE RUINED REMAINS OF FOUR 'GUSUKU' FORTRESSES

BELOW The graceful arcs in the walls of Zakimi Gusuku are part of extensive enclosures which, snake-like, follow the contours of the small hill. The arcs face away from the castle interior, offering protection.

Okinawa's main island is about 70 miles (113 km) long, and in medieval times farming communities developed defence systems against their rivals. By the twelfth century this had led to the construction of fortifications known as *gusuku*, which enclosed dwellings and sacred sites. After the feuding factions coalesced into Three Kingdoms during the fourteenth century, the *gusuku* assumed a vital role as seat of the regional rulers.

Nakijin Castle, fortress for the Northern Kingdom, stands on a hill overlooking the East China Sea and is notable for its size, extending over 14 acres (6 hectares). It was first constructed in the thirteenth century although it was not completed until the early fifteenth. Ongoing excavations have unearthed Chinese connections both in the

RIGHT Among the features of the *gusuku* are stone arched gates that allow access between enclosures. The style of construction is different from Japan's castle architecture, which was a factor in winning World Heritage Site status.

BELOW Zakimi Castle was built in the fifteenth century by the warrior-lord Gosamaru, renowned for his fortifications. The walls are made of Ryukyuan limestone and range in height from 10 to 43 feet (3 to 13 meters).

construction techniques and in the imported pottery. Amongst the present remains are 1 mile (1.6 km) of limestone walls and several *utaki* shrines.

Zakimi Castle was built by a powerful warrior called Gosamaru (d. 1458), who played a key part in the fight for unification. As a reward, he was given charge of Nakijin, which he used as a base while constructing Zakimi to monitor rebel elements in the north. The new fortress had two large enclosures, surrounded by massive walls up to 43 feet (13 meters) high. The remains are of interest for the arched stone gates, a distinctly Okinawan feature, and the unusual graceful curves of the walls.

Katsuren Castle, the oldest of the properties, dates back to the twelfth century and consists of four enclosures set on a slope. Located on a promontory, the site offers attractive views which include sunsets over the Pacific. There are several *utaki* shrines, the most venerated being a tall round stone in the upper enclosure that houses the tutelary deity.

Like Zakimi Castle, Nakagusuku is linked with the warrior Gosamaru, who reconstructed the fourteenth-century castle. It was intended to counter the Katsuren lord, who was a dangerous rival to the king. The castle's enclosures extend along a steep promontory, and although the buildings are gone, the formidable walls remain in good order, testimony to the distinctive stone building skills of the island nation.

ABOVE LEFT The extensive grounds of Nakijin Gusaku were developed over several centuries. The highest ramparts overlook the sea, and it's thought the enclosure in the foreground was used for raising and training horses.

FAR LEFT Various techniques were employed in constructing the *gusuku* walls. These include aligning and stacking unprocessed stones, square-shaped stones and hexagonal stones.

LEFT Katsuren Gusaku, the oldest of Okinawa's World Heritage castles, had four separate enclosures as well as six religious areas, including one for the god of fire which dwelt in the kitchen area.

THE OGASAWARA ISLANDS

A SUBTROPICAL 'GALAPAGOS' OF JAPAN

OGASAWARA ISLANDS AT A GLANCE

REGISTRATION 2011, as 'an outstanding example of the ongoing evolutionary processes in oceanic island ecosystems'.

FEATURES A group of over 30 islands, known in English as the Bonin Islands, of which only Chichijima and Hahajima are inhabited (pop. 2,500).

ACCESS 25 hours by ship from Tokyo. Departure weekly, more often in season.

INFORMATION For prices, sailing schedule and tourist information, check the OgasawaraKaiun website.

DURATION A minimum of 5 days (including 2 days sailing). The two main islands can be toured in half a day each.

ACTIVITIES Eco-tours, night tour, trekking and marine sports such as coral snorkeling, whale watching, swimming with dolphins, etc.

Ogasawara is special in many ways. The islands belong to Tokyo Prefecture although they're some 620 miles (1,000 km) to the south, similar in latitude to Okinawa. Until the 1830s they were uninhabited, being first settled by Westerners and Pacific Islanders, descendants of whom still remain today. Above all, they have unique forms of flora and fauna, which owe themselves to the location. Volcanic in formation, the islands were never joined to the continent in contrast to the rest of Japan, which means that life forms developed distinctive characteristics. It is why scientists have called the islands 'a laboratory for evolution'.

The effects of adaptation are evident in both plant and animal life. Tree leaves have grown smaller and stiffer due to the dry climate. Hermaphrodite flowers have morphed into separate males and females. And there are subspecies of birds found nowhere else, such as the Ogasawara

RIGHT With their remote location, low population and Pacific blues, the islands offer scuba divers perfect conditions for underwater exploration of the coral reefs.

FAR RIGHT The undulating coastline of Chichijima offers fine views and the beaches provide ample opportunity for sunbathing, snorkeling and fishing. The official 'beach opening ceremony' is held on January 1.

OPPOSITE TOP LEFT The Chichijima Marine Center has a hatchery and conservation unit for endangered green turtles. The nearby seas are also host to bottlenose dolphins, humpback whales and manta rays.

OPPOSITE TOP MIDDLE The Ogasawara *mejiro* (White-eye), official bird of the islands, has special characteristics which differ from its counterpart on the mainland.

OPPOSITE TOP RIGHT The Terihahamabou, endemic to Ogasawara, blooms all year round and slowly changes color during the course of the day from yellow to red.

ABOVE Boats can be hired to tour the coasts of the two inhabited islands and also to visit uninhabited islands. The archipelago has over 30 islands altogether, often referred to in English as the Bonin Islands, derived from the Japanese *munin*, meaning 'uninhabited'.

LEFT Thickly wooded fern forests thrive in the subtropical conditions. The *bischofia* in the foreground is considered an invasive species which threatens to overrun native vegetation.

buzzard which is smaller and lighter in color than its mainland counterpart. Scientists say they are able to study here the development of an oceanic island arc that has preserved the process of formation since its origin. The land snail has proved of particular interest, with 94 percent being endemic to the islands, as are 36 percent of the plants and 28 percent of the insects.

The only native mammal is the critically endangered Bonin Flying Fox, a type of fruit bat with eyesight, which numbers around 150 in all. Other mammals have arrived as a result of human habitation, including goats, black rats and feral cats. Unfortunately, they are destructive of the island environment: goats eat up the food supply, including rare plants; rats feed on precious seeds, berries and land snails; cats prey on protected birds (194 species have been spotted altogether on the islands, several of which are extremely rare).

Other destructive aliens include the virulent *bischofia* (bishop wood tree), which takes over native woodland, and a predatory New Guinea flatworm responsible for a reduction in the number of land snails. Conservation measures have been put in place to restore the original balance, including laying poison, setting up bird sanctuaries and capturing the cats. To prevent harmful spores being brought in, all visitors to Ogasawara have their footwear disinfected on arrival, and it was partly due to such protective measures that the islands were granted World Heritage Site registration.

Because of their volcanic origin, there is little flat land on the islands and the hilly terrain is covered by subtropical forest or shrubland. Chichijima (Father Island) is the larger of the two inhabited islands, and its main town caters to tourists (numbers have gone up by a third since World Heritage Site registration). Hahajima (Mother Island), two hours away by ferry, is smaller but hillier than its neighbor, with a population of just 450, mostly huddled around the port.

The World Heritage Site covers all of the islands except for the populated areas, and takes in a small part of the sea. With its coral reefs, warm waters (never below 59 degrees F/15 degrees C) and 'Bonin blue' clarity, the water is a paradise for divers who may get the opportunity to swim among tropical fish, manta rays and dolphins. Giant turtles come here to nest,

RIGHT Ogiike (Ogi Pond) is prized for its 'submerged karst' formation, by which the rock has dissolved into an attractive arch. It lies on the uninhabited Minamijima, only accessible with a registered nature guide.

Ogasawara Islands

500 km
200 miles

N

Sea of Japan

TOKYO

Osaka

Izu Islands

PACIFIC OCEAN

Nishino Shima

Ogasawara Islands

Mukojima Group
Chichijima Group
Hahajima Group

Daito Islands

Kazan Island Group

Kita-iwoto Island
Iwoto Island
Minami-iwoto Island

Minami Torishima
(Marcus Island)

—Okino Torishima

Philippine Sea

Mariana Islands

BELOW The Ogasawara *birou* (Blue Japanese Fan Palm) is a member of the Livistona family and is native to the islands. It has a smaller and thinner trunk than its Chinese equivalent.

BOTTOM The endemic Screw Pine is the official tree of Ogasawara and is commonly known, for obvious reasons, as the Tako no ki (Octopus Tree).

FAR LEFT The Ogasawara Islands are the biggest breeding ground for green turtles in Japan. The creatures lay eggs from June to July, which hatch in August or September.

LEFT The Muninshusuran is an endemic species which grows in dim and moist parts of woodland, with flowers that bloom around December.

BELOW Hahajima (Mother Island) lies 31 miles (50 km) to the south of Chichijima (Father Island). With a dwindling population of just 450, the island does not see much usage of its Kitakou (Northern Port) pictured here. Oki Port is the main harbor.

while humpback and sperm whales can be seen in season. It was here, in fact, that whale watching first began in Japan.

Because of the restricted access, islanders are grateful to those who visit and they show their appreciation in a special kind of send-off. As the ferry to Tokyo pulls out of port, a flotilla of small motorboats accompanies it to open water, with those onboard shouting and waving farewell before diving dramatically into the sea. It makes for a memorable end to a special kind of trip. Not many people are able to get to Ogasawara, but those who take the trouble are soon aware of the distinctive character of the islands. One can see why Nathaniel Savory and his cohorts settled here in the 1840s. Little could they have realised that the land they had made their own would one day be recognised as a unique natural environment and a Japanese World Heritage Site.

TOP Hahajima was first settled by the Englishman James Motley and his Micronesian wife Ketty. Charmed by the delights of places like Minamizaki (Southern Cape), they proved to be pioneers in making a life on the island.

ABOVE As well as special botanical and zoological features, the volcanic archipelago also has unusual rock formations, such as this striking example of pillow lava on Chichijima.

YAKUSHIMA ISLAND

A PRIMEVAL FOREST WITH THOUSAND-YEAR-OLD CEDARS

YAKUSHIMA ISLAND AT A GLANCE

REGISTRATION 1993, for its unique environment and Yakusugi (Yakushima cedars).

ACCESS From Kagoshima in Kyushu by air (30 mins), jetfoil (2 hrs) or ferry (4 hours). Also direct flights from Fukuoka or Osaka Itami.

INFORMATION Tourist Office in Kagoshima (0997) 49-4010 email: info@yakukan.jp. Also Environmental Culture Village (Miyanoura: (0997) 42-2900); World Heritage Conservation Center (Anbo: (0997) 46-2992); Yakusugi Museum (Anbo: (0997) 46-3113).

DURATION At least 2 days, longer if trekking.

ATTRACTIONS Hiking at Yakusugi Land, Shiratani Unsuikyo and to the Jomon cedar. Also diving, hot springs and waterfalls.

The small island of Yakushima (pop. 17,000) lies 37 miles (60 kilometers) south of the larger island of Kyushu. It has the highest mountain in the region, Mt Miyanoura, which is 6,348 feet (1,935 meters). Several others are over 5,900 feet (1,800 meters). It is not only the wettest place in the whole of Japan but it is also the most southerly to have snow. The sea, on the other hand, is relatively warm because of the current flowing from the South China coast, so that even in winter the ocean temperature does not fall below 66 degrees Fahrenheit (19 Centigrade).

Because of the steepness of the mountains, the vegetation on Yakushima ranges from the subalpine to the subtropical within a few miles. As a result, there is a huge diversity of flora with some 1,900 species, of which 94 are endemic. What

makes the island so distinctive is that for many plants this is their most southerly point of distribution, while for others it is their most northerly. And among the 16 mammals on the island are the Yaku monkey and Yaku deer, which have

OPPOSITE Water is of the essence to Yakushima's lush vegetation, and thanks to the island's mountains there is no shortage of rainfall. According to a local saying, it rains 35 days a month.

ABOVE RIGHT The World Heritage Site covers the mountainous middle of the island, extending as far as the coast in the west. The road connecting the main ports of Miyanoura in the north and Anbo in the east continues on to the south where there are waterfalls and seaside hot springs.

RIGHT Hiking through Yakushima's woods takes one into a wonderland of twisted roots and gnarled trunks. The verdant surroundings are an absorbing showpiece of nature's ability to create unlikely shapes and formations.

ABOVE The Jomonsugi is the pride of Yakushima, being the largest and oldest of the cedars. A round-trip hike takes 8–10 hours and viewing is restricted to a distant platform. Its discovery in 1968 led to moves to protect the forests and also initiated ecotourism.

RIGHT The heart mark of Wilson's Stump is a popular feature. Felled in the 1500s, the tree is named after an English botanist, E. H. Wilson, who rediscovered it in the 1900s. The timber is believed to have been used for Hoko-ji in Kyoto.

evolved different characteristics from their mainland counterparts.

It is the giant cedars, however, for which the island is famous. Cedars normally live for about 500 years, but because of the high rainfall and humidity in Yakushima the trees produce resin which protects them against rotting. As a result, Yaku cedars grow to dimensions not seen elsewhere and the shapes can leave one gasping in amazement. Gnarled and twisted like grotesque creations of the imagination, the trees are host to

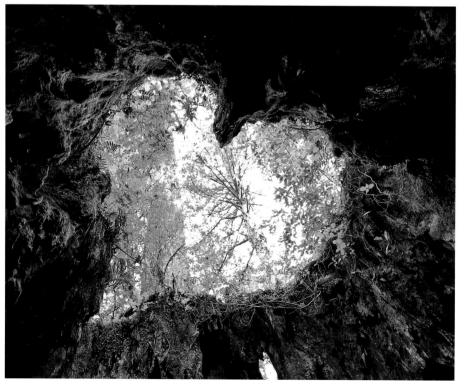

numerous parasites, with shrubs and saplings springing out of their tops and sides. There are skeleton trees, too, on the exposed mountain sides, stripped of their bark by fierce winds but eerily alive.

The most famous of the trees is the Jomonsugi (Jomon Cedar), named after one of Japan's prehistoric periods (15,000–300 BC). Estimates of its age vary from 2,000 up to 7,000 years old, around the time that human habitation would have begun on the island. The giant cryptomeria is 83 feet (25 meters) tall with a gigantic trunk 53 feet (16 meters) in circumference, making it not only the oldest but the biggest conifer in Japan. It is the island's prime attraction, requiring a round-trip hike of 8–10 hours over challenging terrain. For conservation purposes, visitors are restricted to a platform 49 feet (15 meters) distant, and though the trek is usually done in a day, there are huts for camping overnight.

For those who prefer something less rigorous, there are two other options to view the cedars. One is at Yakusugi Land,

which offers the easiest terrain with flattened pathways, hand rails and a mixed forest of fresh-flowing streams and moss-covered floors. There are four overlapping courses, which rise in difficulty and length from 30 to 150 minutes. Notable cedars are identified like exhibits in a museum, and the names are self-explanatory: the Twins, Mother and Child, the Arch Cedar.

More demanding is the Shiratani Unsuikyo Ravine, where the hikes range from one to four hours. The simplest course leads to the Yayoisugi (Yayoi Cedar), named after another prehistoric age (300

LEFT TOP Yaku monkeys are smaller than their mainland counterparts and are regarded as a subspecies. There are some 7,000 in all, nearly half the human population.

LEFT Mt Miyanoura is the highest of the island's mountains, and because of the dramatic rise from sea level, vegetation characteristic of areas between Kyushu and Hokkaido can be seen within a short distance.

BELOW The warm temperate broad-leaved forests of Yakushima have survived, whereas many others in Japan were felled due to population pressure. Protecting the island's woods from increased tourism has become a major concern.

BC–AD 250). The woods here are thick and verdant, with ferns and carpets of moss. (The forest served as inspiration for the Hayao Miyazaki animated film, *Princess Mononoke* (1997).) The longest of the hikes, which becomes steep and rigorous in parts, leads to the Taikoiwa Rock from which there are appealing views.

Although it is possible to get around Yakushima Island on the infrequent buses, a rental car is the only means of seeing the World Heritage west coast. Apart from the Yaku cedars, the island also offers hot springs and waterfalls, while the Environmental Cultural Village Center provides a spectacular overview on a huge screen. In June or July, loggerhead turtles come to nest. The steamy summer season is best avoided. Istead, in spring or autumn hiking provides a journey back in time— back to the primeval woods of prehistory.

OPPOSITE ABOVE LEFT Yakusugi Land is a nature park with four hiking courses of differing lengths and difficulty. The trails offer a chance to sample the island's forests, including mountain streams, moss-covered rocks and, of course, giant Yaku cedars.

OPPOSITE ABOVE RIGHT Venerable members of Yakusugi Land, such as the Buddhasugi pictured here, have nearby noticeboards giving details. This particular tree is 1,800 years old, 26 feet (8 meters) in circumference and just over 70 feet (21.5 meters) in height.

OPPOSITE BELOW The shorter courses at Yakusugi Land are well paved with wood or stone. Since felling took place about 300 years ago, there are plenty of open spaces, tree stumps and young growth to offer variety.

TOP The Shiratani Unsui Ravine, 30 minutes by bus from Miyanoura Port, offers several hiking trails, the longest of which takes four hours and leads past Taikoiwa Rock with its commanding views.

ABOVE The Satsuki Suspension Bridge in Shiratani Unsuikyo connects the relatively easy Yayoisugi course with more rigorous trails that lead to other Yaku cedars. Part of the forest here was the inspiration for the 1997 animated film, *Princess Mononoke*.

SHIRAKAMI SANCHI

THE LAST OF JAPAN'S GREAT VIRGIN BEECH FORESTS

SHIRAKAMI SANCHI AT A GLANCE

REGISTRATION 1993, as 'the last remaining virgin stand of Siebold's beech forest'.

FEATURES A National Park with thickly wooded mountains, waterfalls and lakes.

ACCESS From Tokyo, train to Hirosaki in Aomori Prefecture (about 4 hrs), or Noshiro in Akita Prefecture (about 5 hrs). Limited bus access. Rental car recommended.

INFORMATION Shirakami Sanchi Visitor Center (50 mins by bus from Hirosaki) has an exhibition and 30-mins large screen film. Nature guides available. Tel. (0172) 85 2810; fax (0172) 85 2833. See also http://school. shirakami.gr.jp/en/guide.htm.

DURATION At least 2 days, longer if hiking or camping

ATTRACTIONS Juniko (Twelve Lakes), Anmon Falls, nature trails, angling. Panoramic views from the Resort Shirakami train. Autumn colors recommended.

Shirakami Sanchi is a mountainous area that contains one of the world's largest virgin beech forests, a remnant of the cool temperate woods of ancient times. Once prevalent throughout Japan, beeches were logged or fell prey to land development, but Shirakami was spared because of its rugged nature. Gorges, waterfalls and steeply sided mountains, several over 3,280 feet (1,000 meters), characterize the terrain, which straddles the border of Akita and Aomori Prefectures in northern Honshu.

Northwest Japan has one of the heaviest snowfalls in the world, and the branches of the Siebold beech (named after a German botanist) are able to cope with the weight better than other trees. The tree can grow up to 82 feet (25 meters), has a lifespan of 250–300 years and helps sustain a fertile environment. Not only do its nuts have a high nutrient value but its moisture-retaining leaves create a sponge like covering on the forest floor in which insects thrive. These form an important part of the food chain and a remarkable 2,212 species have been identified.

In the 1980s, the area came under threat when large-scale construction work began on a road but it was stopped thanks to a protest movement. World Heritage recognition shortly afterwards helped seal conservation of the core area (the UNESCO site comprises roughly a third of the mountains). Around it is a National Park, with open access to woodland, waterfalls, lakes and springs.

Because of its untouched nature, the site has been called a 'forest museum'. Over 500 plant species and 27 bird species have been found here and amongst the flora are several rare flowers.

RIGHT Beech woods create particularly fertile environments, at the same time providing high moisture retention and strong erosion resistance. An hour-long nature trail at the Okuakaishi Beech Woods in the north offers a chance to experience the conditions.

OPPOSITE The Shirakami Mountains, characterized by jagged valleys and steep gorges, are an important water catchment. Picturesque in autumn, the rivers turn into tumbling torrents when winter snows melt, making it a popular area with anglers.

Some of the animals are also unusual, such as the Japanese serow and the black woodpecker, of which there are thought to be only 50 surviving. Mammals found include the black bear, smaller in size than its brown cousin in Hokkaido, but unusually for Honshu there are no deer or wild boar owing to the volume of snow.

Seasonal differences are striking. The high altitude means that winters are long, but with the melting snows of spring small flowers appear and the black bear wakes from hibernation. In May, new growth becomes apparent and the sound of woodpeckers rings through the woods. By summer butterflies can be seen, while monkeys play amongst the honeysuckle. Come autumn, when the leaves turn brown and yellow, mushrooms proliferate as squirrels and birds gorge themselves on beech nuts. With the cold Siberian winds of winter, the woods grow quiet

ABOVE From the viewing platform at the Blue Pond (Aoike), visitors can look down into the clear blue water and see the eerie shapes of fallen trees looming in the depths below.

BELOW LEFT Although Blackbear Falls (Kurokuma no Taki) lies outside the World Heritage Site, its waters originate there. Ranked among Japan's top 100 waterfalls, the name is thought to derive from its resemblance in shape to a standing bear.

BELOW The Mother Tree, a symbol of Shirakami Sanchi, is the oldest beech tree in the area and is believed to be 400 years old. It stands not far from the Anmon Falls on the Shirakami Line, an unpaved route to the north of the mountains offering fine views.

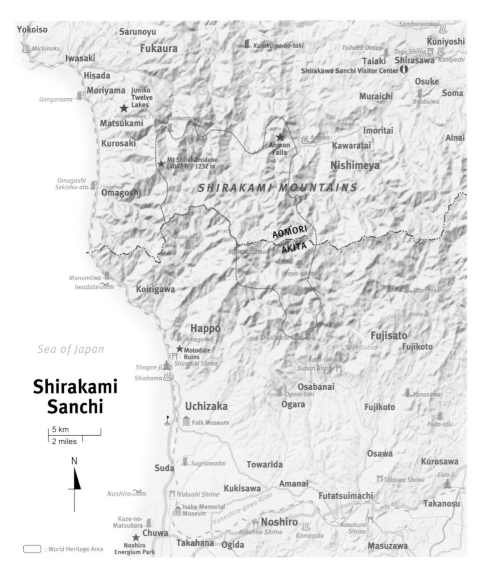

and animals which don't hibernate find it hard to survive. Only the smoke from charcoal huts speaks of life at all in the barren whiteness. The area is all but inaccessible from November to March.

Shirakami's best-known attraction are the Juniko (Twelve Lakes), which lie near the coast outside the designated World Heritage area. The most popular is Aoike (Blue Pond), where the unusual color of the water makes the submerged trees seem otherworldly. Over on the eastern side, within the UNESCO site, are the three-layered Anmon Falls, 85, 121 and 138 feet respectively (26, 37 and 42 meters). The riverside path leading to them runs through beech forest and under rock cliffs, becoming steeper as it nears the final fall.

For those seeking a bigger challenge, there are opportunities for hiking and climbing. In the south, a short but steep trail leads up Mt Futatsumori, while Mt Shirakamidake, at 4,042 feet (1,232 meters), is the tallest mountain and a tough climb. There is a hut for overnighting. Most visitors, however, are content to see it all from a car (three unpaved roads cross the mountains), or to ride on the Resort Shirakami train which allows panoramic views of mountains and coastline. Sunsets over the Sea of Japan can be particularly spectacular. It would be a shame, though, to leave it at that, for entering the woods provides a rare chance to experience Japan just as it would have been 5,000–8,000 years ago—in the Jomon Age (12000–300 BC).

TOP Shirakami is home to rare animals, one of which, the Serow (Kamoshika), is peculiar to Japan. Herbivorous in nature, it is believed to have served in primeval times as a type of cattle.

ABOVE The life cycle in the mountains depends on the forest–river–sea interaction. Rain is carried by streams down to the sea, where evaporation leads to clouds forming, which empty themselves back onto the mountain forests.

RIGHT Because beech has a particularly good water retention rate, the woods are home to many kinds of herbs and fungi. Deciding which ones are edible can be a risky business.

SHIRETOKO PENINSULA

A VERY SPECIAL ECOSYSTEM IN JAPAN'S FAR NORTH

SHIRETOKO PENINSULA AT A GLANCE

REGISTRATION 2005, because it represents 'an outstanding example of the interaction of marine and terrestrial ecosystems'.

FEATURES A peninsula with volcanic mountain spine and coastal cliffs. Goko (Five Lakes), waterfalls, hot springs, mountain pass.

ACCESS From the town of Utoro in northeast Hokkaido, 2 hrs by bus from Memanbetsu Airport or 50 mins by bus from JR Shiretoko Shari stn. Rental car recommended.

DURATION 3 or 4 days to take in different aspects, longer if hiking.

INFORMATION Shiretoko Tourist Information (0152) 23-2424. Rausu Tourist Information (0153) 87-3330. For guides and tours, Nature Center (0152) 24-2114; email: info@shiretoko. or.jp. May–July reservations needed for Goko (Five Lakes): see www.goko.go.jp/english

ACTIVITIES Hiking, eco-tours, boat trips, whale watching, fishing.

OPPOSITE ABOVE LEFT Shiretoko has one of the world's highest population densities of brown bear. At the Five Lakes, measures are in place to ensure the safety of visitors. This picture was taken from the platformed pathway to Lake One.

OPPOSITE ABOVE MIDDLE The Steller's Sea Eagle comes from the Russian Far East to winter at Shiretoko. It is the heaviest eagle in the world and can have a wing span of over 6.6 feet (2 meters).

OPPOSITE ABOVE RIGHT The Ezo Deer, larger than its Honshu cousin, has thrived in recent years. Although some see it as a pest, hunting and killing is prohibited within the Wildlife Protection Area.

OPPOSITE BELOW The Five Lakes are Shiretoko's prime venue, offering fine views and a safe environment. They lie in primeval forest, but here the Second Lake opens up to allow sight of the Shiretoko Mountain Range.

Seaside cliffs, spectacular waterfalls and beautiful lakes. It is the image many have of the Shiretoko Peninsula but there is more to it than that. Because it is the most southerly area in the northern hemisphere to have sea ice, it has an unusual diversity of wildlife. The mountains that form the spine of the peninsula, which include two active volcanoes, also ensure a diversity of flora, ranging from alpine plants to coastal flowers. Moreover, it's a bird watcher's paradise with 256 different species spotted, including the endangered Steller's Sea Eagle. For those who think Japan is only urban sprawl and crowded cities, Shiretoko is the perfect antidote.

The environment owes itself to the fresh water emptied by the River Amur into the Sea of Okhotsk, lowering the salt content in the upper levels. In winter, the water turns into drift ice, which carries a type of plankton known as 'ice algae'. When this melts, the nutrients provide food for an abundance of small fish, which in turn attract birds and sea mammals. The surviving salmon and sea trout make their way up rivers to spawn, where they are fed upon by terrestrial life, such as bears.

The area's main attraction is a group of Five Lakes (Goko) just north of the hot spring town of Utoro. Relatively small, they are connected by a trail nearly 2 miles (3 km) long, which takes about 90 minutes to walk. In season, visitors are given a short talk in preparation: 'This is the home of the bears, and humans are the guests.' The message is that avoidance is better than encounter, which is why

many people carry bells or call out when walking through the woods.

Should a bear be sighted, the trail is closed off and visitors are restricted to the elevated pathway that leads to a viewpoint overlooking Lake No. 1. There are 200 brown bears in the area, making it one of the earth's most densely populated for the creature. Females weigh around 440 pounds (200 kg), males up to twice as much. However, the animals are 90 percent vegetarian and unlikely to attack without provocation, so 'Don't panic, keep calm, and slowly back away' is the advice. Easier said than done!

There are thirty-three other mammals in the National Park, including rarely seen species such as the Japanese Red Fox. Ezo Deer, on the other hand, with their distinctive white flecks, are ubiquitous. They were almost hunted to death after the opening up of Hokkaido in the nineteenth century, but now with 10,000 in all there is talk of overpopulation, for they strip bark and eat grassland flowers.

The best way to see the peninsula is from the sea, for it affords views of inaccessible sites. On the wetter and windier east coast, there are boats out of Rausu to view whales, dolphins and sea lions (on a clear day, the disputed Russian islands too), while afterwards one can

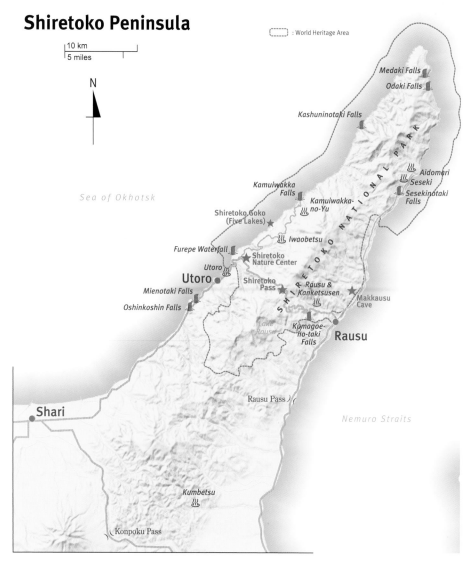

Shiretoko Peninsula

ABOVE From Utoro a road runs north to the Five Lakes and Kamuiwakka Falls. The road to Rausu leads over the Shiretoko Pass and is closed in winter. The west coast is best seen by boat out of Utoro.

LEFT Drift ice covers the Okhotsk Sea in winter, though not the Japan Sea or the Pacific. With it comes an abundance of phytoplankton and Sea Angels (*clione*). In late March, the sea serves also as the birthplace for spotted seals.

OPPOSITE ABOVE The viewing platform at the first of the Five Lakes faces the Shiretoko Range, which was formed by volcanic activity 250,000 years ago; two active volcanoes still remain. Mt Rausu, tallest of the mountains at 5,446 feet (1,660 meters), has climbing routes from either side.

OPPOSITE BELOW Water sprays from the Oshinkoshin Falls, just south of Utoro. Ranked among Japan's top 100, it is just one of several picturesque waterfalls on the Shiretoko Peninsula, particularly along the coast where rivers plunge over cliffs and straight into the sea.

bask in open-air hot springs. The popular option, though, is the three-hour trip from Utoro, which sails along the west coast past cliffside waterfalls, including the unusual Fureppe Falls to which no river leads; it is fed by an underground stream. The ships go all the way up to the tip of the cape, which is off-limits to visitors by land, and in the right season bears can be seen at the river mouths catching fish.

For the adventurous, there are mountain hiking trails and camp sites; for nature lovers and bird watchers, there are specialist eco-tours. Most prefer to visit by car, however, and the road that goes part of the way up the peninsula leads past the hot-spring Kamuiwakka Falls, where one can wade up the levels to bathe in the uppermost basin. There's also a pleasant drive over the mountain pass connecting the coasts (closed in winter), where one can stop off to walk to Rausu Lake or Kumagoe Waterfall. Winter offers a wonderland of snow and a chance to see the amazing drift ice. Shiretoko may not compare with Himalayan heights for spectacle, but the peninsula has a charm of its own. Here, it is said, is Japan's last sanctuary for endangered species and a rare chance to experience nature in the raw.

Additional Sites in Japan Nominated for World Heritage Status

A Tentative List consists of places that are being prepared by their respective country for nomination as a World Heritage Site. Inclusion on the Tentative List is a necessary precondition in the process of registration, and at the time of writing there are twelve sites on Japan's list ranging in type from ancient burial mounds to nineteenth-century industrial works. The sites below are listed according to the year of inscription on the list.

Kamakura Big Buddha

1) Temples, Shrines and Other Structures of Ancient Kamakura (1992)

From 1185 to 1333 Kamakura was the seat of authority in Japan. It marked the coming to power of the warrior class, whose rule continued until 1867, and the proposed site comprises properties related to the samurai. The city had natural defences, with hills on three sides and the Pacific to the south. Within the folds of the topography were built temples, particularly Zen, and at the center stood the prestigious Shinto shrine of Tsurugaoka Hachiman-gu. Along with these, the proposal includes Kamakura's free-standing Great Buddha as well as samurai houses, a former port, and the steep pathways that led from the city to the outside world.

2) Hikone Castle (1992)

Hikone Castle was built from 1604 to 1624 during a Golden Age of castle architecture in Japan. The complex is centered on a hill facing Lake Biwa, and its three moats once enclosed an inner, outer and residential district. The well-preserved structures include gateways, turrets, stables and a three-storey donjon with elaborate roofing. In addition, there are palace-style buildings and gardens. During the Edo Period (1603–1868) the castle belonged to the powerful Ii family and played a strategic role in maintaining Tokugawa rule in the region. Following the Meiji Restoration of 1868, it survived the destruction of castles to become a striking reminder of the former samurai culture.

Hikone Castle

3) The Tomioka Silk Mill and Related Industrial Heritage (2007)

Built in 1872, the Tomioka Silk Mill in Gunma Prefecture helped boost production of Japan's raw silk, making it a major export for the emerging country. French technology was employed, typifying the rapid modernisation of Meiji Japan, in conjunction with innovations such as the mass production of cocoons. As a result, the surrounding area saw the development of mulberry farms, silkworm raising houses and the transportation of cocoons. The result was a 'cultural landscape' based on the life cycle of the silk worm. Led in this way by Tomioka, Japan had by 1909 become the world's largest exporter of raw silk.

4) Asuka-Fujiwara: Archaeological Sites of Japan's Ancient Capitals and Related Properties (2007)

In the Asuka Period (592–710), Japan emerged as a centralised state, and the words *tenno* (emperor) and *Nihon* (Japan) date from this time. A major feature of the proposal is the excavated site of Japan's first capital city, Fujiwara-kyo (694–710), together with the three sacred hills that surrounded it. Other items consist of burial mounds and the remains of wooden buildings related to the imperial élite. The period also saw the development of Buddhism in Japan, which is reflected in the remains of early temples, including those of the country's very first Buddhist building, Asuka-dera.

5) Churches and Christian Sites in Nagasaki (2007)

The properties in this proposal relate to 400 years of Christianity, from its introduction in 1549 up to World War II. At first the European religion enjoyed considerable success, but during the early seventeenth century it was brutally suppressed and thought to have been eliminated. However, pockets of Hidden Christians continued to practise in secret, particularly in the Nagasaki region where Jesuit missionaries had once had their base. Following Japan's opening to the West in the 1850s, churches were erected in a mix of European and Japanese styles, many of which stand on or near sites associated with Hidden Christian worship and the persecution of earlier times.

6) The Main Building of the National Museum of Western Art (2007)

The Main Building of the museum is the sole example in East Asia of work by the famed architect Le Corbusier. It was built in 1959 to house the Matsukata Collection, put together by a Japanese industrialist prior to World War II. Stored in Paris, the collection was confiscated by France during the war and handed back in 1953 with the stipulation that it be suitably housed. The result was a three-storey structure (one underground) made of reinforced concrete and designed as a spiral within a square. Characteristic Le Corbusier features include pilotis (piers), a roof garden, ramps and a striking use of natural light.

Oura Church, Nagasaki

7) Okinoshima Island and Related Sites in Munakata Region (2009)

Okinoshima is a sacred island north of Kyushu, inhabited by a single Shinto representative. From the fourth to the tenth century, rituals for safety at sea were conducted there in conjunction with trade missions to the continent. Over 80,000 offerings have been unearthed, indicating its importance. The proposal also includes properties in Northern Kyushu related to the Munakata clan, who were in charge of the island rituals. These consist of the Tsuyazaki tumuli where clan members are buried, as well as the Munakata Grand Shrine honoring the three clan *kami*. Up to today, the shrine maintains the island's sanctity, which remains off-limits to women.

Jomon huts (reconstructed), Aomori

8) The Modern Industrial Heritage Sites in Kyushu and Yamaguchi (2009)

Japan's emergence onto the world stage after 1868 was remarkable for being the first time that a non-Western country achieved rapid industrialisation. The Kyushu and Yamaguchi areas played a leading part in this, particularly in terms of iron, steel, coal mines and shipbuilding. The listed properties illustrate how Western technology was adopted and integrated into the local culture. These include former factories, coal mines and furnaces, together with the site of a one-time shipyard. In addition to the core area, two districts in Honshu are included because of their close association in historical and technical terms.

9) Jomon Archaeological Sites in Hokkaido, Northern Tohoku and Other Regions (2009)

From around 13000 BC to 300 BC there existed in Japan a type of Neolithic culture known as Jomon. Although the people engaged in hunting, fishing and gathering, they lived in permanent settlements near their food sources—along sea coasts, rivers and the edge of deciduous forests. Their lifestyle was adapted to the environment and to the humid temperate climate that followed the ending of the Ice Age. Amongst the site's components are shell mounds, stone circles and the archaeological remains of villages. Excavated items include cord-patterned Jomon pottery and the extraordinary clay figurines known as *dogu*.

Hashima Island (Gunkanjima), Nagasaki

Takkoku no Iwaya at Hiraizumi

10) Mozu-Furuichi Kofungun Ancient Tumulus Clusters (2010)

There are more than 200,000 burial mounds in Japan dating from the late third century to the early seventh. Constructed for the families of the ruling élite, they vary in size and shape. The largest are the immense keyhole-shaped mounds of the Osaka Plain, where there are two major clusters comprising approximately 90 tumuli. These include the Nintoku Tumulus, built in Sakai City. Osaka Prefecture, which is the largest burial mound in the world in terms of circumference, as well as twelve others measuring over 656 feet (200 meters) in length. Funeral accessories such as mirrors, jewelry and iron implements were buried with the clan chiefs. The *haniwa* clay figures of humans, animals, buildings and other items which stood along the outside are displayed at museums and show the importance of continental exchange at this time.

11) The Sado Complex of Heritage Mines (2010)

On the island of Sado in the Japan Sea are the remains of mining production which date back to the mid-sixteenth century, when imported techniques for surveying and smelting helped develop the largest gold and silver mine in Japan.

The historical structures, archaeological sites and mining settlements are among the best preserved in East Asia. The Sado mines not only underpinned the introduction of a gold coinage system but were given cultural expression in picture scrolls and Noh plays. Following the Meiji Restoration of 1868, they played a leading part in modernisation through the speedy introduction of Western technology, such as vertical shaft mining.

12) Hiraizumi Temples, Gardens and Archaeological Sites Representing the Buddhist Pure Land (extension) (2012)

Hiraizumi already has five properties registered as part of its World Heritage Site, and it is seeking to add a further five related to the Pure Land estates of the twelfth century. Among the proposed additions are the excavated sites of temples, the former administrative center of the area and the archaeological remains of a large manor from which came the provisions to sustain the Pure Land enterprise. Also nominated is a cliffside temple, Takkoku no Iwaya, featuring a rock carving of Buddha and a platform-style building, which once played an important politico-religious role in Hiraizumi's links with Kyoto.

ACKNOWLEDGMENTS

For the opportunity to travel to all 17 World Heritage Sites, my gratitude to Eric Oey of Tuttle and to Ryukoku University for their backing. For acting as occasional chauffeur, companion and research assistant, I owe an enormous debt of thanks to Yuriko Suzuki. Several others provided valuable input, notably Julie Highmore and Paul Carty who generously looked over the manuscript. Michael Wilkins offered technical expertise with computer problems, Micah Gempel provided camera tips, and John Wells handled digital matters with great patience. A special note of thanks must go to John Einarsen of the *Kyoto Journal*, who not only offered support but enabled me to attend the conference celebrating the 40th Anniversary of the World Heritage Convention in Kyoto. It provided an opportunity to interact with some of the world's leading experts, facilitated by Kadokura Toshiaki of Japan's Foreign Ministry and Gina Doubleday of the World Heritage Center. Finally, mention should be made of the helpful folk at Tuttle, particularly June Chong who eased the way through the design and correction stages. It was a pleasure to work with a publishing firm which still maintains 'old-fashioned values' and a concern with quality.

PHOTO CREDITS

INDEX

THE TUTTLE STORY
"BOOKS TO SPAN THE EAST AND WEST"

Many people are surprised to learn that the world's leading publisher of books on Asia had humble beginnings in the tiny American state of Vermont. The company's founder, Charles E. Tuttle, belonged to a New England family steeped in publishing.

Immediately after WWII, Tuttle served in Tokyo under General Douglas MacArthur and was tasked with reviving the Japanese publishing industry. He later founded the Charles E. Tuttle Publishing Company, which thrives today as one of the world's leading independent publishers.

Though a westerner, Tuttle was hugely instrumental in bringing a knowledge of Japan and Asia to a world hungry for information about the East. By the time of his death in 1993, Tuttle had published over 6,000 books on Asian culture, history and art—a legacy honored by the Japanese emperor with the "Order of the Sacred Treasure," the highest tribute Japan can bestow upon a non-Japanese.

With a backlist of 1,500 titles, Tuttle Publishing is more active today than at any time in its past—inspired by Charles Tuttle's core mission to publish fine books to span the East and West and provide a greater understanding of each.